ATELIER DESHAUS
2001–2020

ATELIER DESHAUS 2001–2020

PARK BOOKS

FOREWORD	OCULUS AND ZEPPELIN by Yung Ho Chang		4
ESSAY	FROM STRUCTURE TO LANGUAGE by Li Xiangning		6
ESSAY	THE RETURN OF THE LITERATI by Li Shiqiao		16

2003–2005	01	XIAYU KINDERGARTEN	36
2006–2008	02	R&D CENTER IN JISHAN SOFTWARE PARK IN NANJING	44
2008–2010	03	KINDERGARTEN IN JIADING NEW TOWN	52
2009–2012	04	QINGPU YOUTH CENTER	62
2009–2011	05	SPIRAL GALLERY I	72
2010–2015	06	SIAC R&D CENTER IN JIADING	80
2010–2015	07	TAO LI YUAN SCHOOL IN JIADING	90
2011–2014	08	LONG MUSEUM WEST BUND	98
2013–2015	09	HUAXIN CONFERENCE HUB	114
2014–2017	10	ONE FOUNDATION KINDERGARTEN	122

2014–2015	11	ATELIER DESHAUS OFFICE ON WEST BUND	134
2015–2019	12	YUNYANG RIVERFRONT VISITOR CENTER	142
2015	13	BLOSSOM PAVILION	154
2015–2019	14	TAIZHOU CONTEMPORARY ART MUSEUM	162
2015–2016	15	MODERN ART MUSEUM SHANGHAI AND ITS WALKWAYS	176
2015–2016	16	TEA HOUSE IN LI GARDEN	194
2015–2017	17	80,000-TON SILOS ART CENTER	204
2016–2021	18	QINTAI ART MUSEUM	216
2017–2018	19	HOUSE ATO	230
2018–2019	20	RIVERSIDE PASSAGE	238
INDEX		CATALOG OF FEATURED WORKS	254
ALL		CATALOG OF WORKS	259
		APPENDIX	274

Yung Ho Chang

OCULUS & ZEPPELIN
DESHAUS: A QUICK SKETCH

I have known Liu Yichun and his business partner Chen Yifeng for so long that I don't recall when we first met. In 2018, however, we had adjacent pavilions at an exhibition in Beijing entitled *House Vision China*, and so we became neighbors for a period of time. On the opening day of the show, Yichun invited me over to the Deshaus pavilion—officially known as House ATO—and offered me a tour that ended on the upper level under an oculus.

OCULUS

A circular skylight topped the extremely thin, tent-shaped roof of "des Haus." Despite the modest size of the temporary project, this skyward-facing aperture possibly constituted something of a Pantheon moment, and more. I didn't bother to ask Yichun if he had been thinking of the great Roman monument when he designed this experimental dwelling for the future. If he did, it wasn't about making a historic reference anyway; and if he didn't, his understanding of architecture as a body of knowledge would enable him to carefully embrace and consider any tectonic element with an open mind and a critical eye. It is not hard to see a sense of refinement in the work of this Shanghai-based architectural office, but it is equally apparent that good taste and modern style are not enough. Deshaus sees itself as a practice that approaches architecture as poetic construction, which means that it takes paramount care of the way a building is put together. This is admittedly not a new position, but rather what architects, builders, and artisans from around the world have been doing throughout the ages. One only needs to look at Fo Guang Si (the Temple of Buddha's Light), which was constructed during the Tang Dynasty, or the Pantheon in Rome, to imagine that. Unfortunately, in the present day that fine and long tradition is losing its momentum all too quickly. I believe that Yichun and Yifeng are among the few surviving—for lack of a better word—"hard-boiled" architects today. Indeed, I clearly remember Yichun's excitement when he shared some of the "secrets" of in-situ concrete with me that he had discovered while working on Long Museum West Bund in Shanghai. But I don't want to be misleading: Yichun is by no means a technician, and I already mentioned the words "poetic" and "eye" above. In my flashback, he and I were still standing under the oculus—the architectural eye, as it were—and looking out. Yichun was searching for something; what specifically I didn't know, but I did know that the duo wouldn't be happy if they saw something repeated, perhaps a familiar device or a design they already knew about. They want to invent.

ZEPPELIN

Yichun has no problem articulating his thoughts, although he is usually a man of few words, none of which are rhetorical. While standing underneath that circular piece of cobalt blue as it turned ever darker, we briefly talked about what we would love to see up there, and agreed on one object: a Zeppelin. Neither of us offered any explanation as to why it should be an airship. That evening, Yichun sent me a perfectly Photoshopped image via WeChat: It was a Zeppelin flying past the oculus right in front of our gaze. Now the question of "why" is posed once more. Since Deshaus is the subject of this short piece, I might try to come up with a couple of possible scenarios for Yichun: Was he imagining a building that can actually fly? Probably not. I don't think he is into anything that fanciful. How about a castle in the air? As Henry David Thoreau once said: "If you have built castles in the air, your work need not be lost; that is where they should be. Now put the foundations under them."

I'm not in the least surprised by Thoreau's statement: Essentially, the idea comes first, followed by substantiation. After all, he did have the experience of building something, namely a cabin near Walden Pond. I hope it is acceptable to label Thoreau an idealist with pragmatic footings, and in fact to describe all good architects, including Yichun, as such. In "Oculus," I presented him as an architect with a thorough grounding in the culture of making; in "Zeppelin," I am tempted to peel off his gentle, quiet facade to reveal a Quixotic heart, which is passionate about ideas and envisions a Brave New World in architectural terms—perhaps one that is futuristic or almost weightless from time to time, with no room for nostalgia. Ultimately, a castle, which is a type of structure dating back to the Middle Ages, seems to be the wrong term for Yichun. It might be more accurate to portray him as an intellectual architect: someone who is well cultivated and informed, both culturally and socially engaging. Bearing that cause in mind, he would deconstruct the Chinese character *she*—which means house and is the second word of the firm's name in Chinese, namely *da she* or "big house"—so that the old can marry the new to produce a structural diagram or allow a Mies-inspired plan to be transformed into vaulted space so that the Modern can meet the Classical. Hence I would suggest that both Yichun and Yifeng are at the same time highly global and highly local—local to Shanghai, local to China—just as critical-minded contemporaries ought to be. I don't believe there is any such thing as a 100 percent thoroughbred these days. I do believe one must have learned to be cosmopolitan, and Yichun and Yifeng have both done that. Back under the oculus, we were staring at the night sky by that point. My Zeppelin came to mind from the world created by François Schuiten in his graphic novels, in which the past, present, and future are always mixed up and populated with figures wrapped in Renaissance robes and riding in winged flying machines. The craft Yichun was mentally engineering must have been built with structural members that had cross-sectional dimensions never exceeding five centimeters. It was about to land in a new reality, beautifully ruinous (perhaps in the spirit of *Blade Runner*?) and just emerging on the horizon, upon which, I assumed, his eyes were fixed.

Li Xiangning
FROM STRUCTURE TO LANGUAGE: THE ARCHITECTURE OF DESHAUS

Contemporary Chinese architecture recalls, as it were, the modern development of the West, expressed in particular through its reacquaintance with the language of modernism. Built on these foundations, it also goes hand in hand with architects becoming more self-aware and recognizing the value of Chinese traditional culture. Whether the aim is to localize the language of modern or contemporary architecture by Le Corbusier, Louis Kahn, or Rem Koolhaas, or to update the intellectual resources of, for example, traditional Chinese timber constructions and garden spaces, in combination with an attitude toward nature that is adapted to local conditions, the result is an architecture that is both inherently contemporary and Chinese. As the British newspaper *The Guardian* commented on the Chinese pavilion's exhibition at the 2018 Venice Biennale: "It cements China's transition from being a playground to the whims of foreign architects, to an emerging architectural powerhouse of sensitive, contextual architecture in its own right."

Given this context, the works realized by Atelier Deshaus cannot be overlooked in any conversation on Chinese architecture today. Thanks to its tireless pursuit of the cultural through works that investigate the relationships between structure, materiality, and form, Deshaus has become a flagbearer for the country's contemporary architectural scene. The firm has subtly reconciled the normative language of modernism with one that hails from China or, more precisely, from the cultural DNA of Shanghai and the Jiangnan region, shaping a unique ambience characterized by elegance and refinement. At the same time, and in sharp contrast to the works created by more conventional architectural offices, Deshaus has contributed exceptional value to Chinese architecture, design, and contemporary culture by embracing research and theoretical discourse on contemporary art, installations, and architectural culture.

FROM DESHAUS TO 大舍
When architects name their firms, they often hope that it might reflect a certain kind of attitude towards architecture while also being fun and memorable. Wang Shu named his studio Amateur while Yung Ho Chang went for Feichang Jianzhu, both expressing a kind of cultural positioning that consciously maintains a distance from the mainstream architectural profession and its works in China. As early as 1993, Liu Yichun was already using Deshaus as a name for the firm he set up with two colleagues at Guangzhou Design Institute. Some years afterwards,

in 2000, when the three founders Liu Yichun, Chen Yifeng, and Zhuang Shen decided to leave the state-owned Tongji Design Institute to establish their own private and independent design office, they continued to call themselves Deshaus. This rather unusual name—especially for a Chinese architectural office—has its roots in the German language, undoubtedly in reference to the three architects' educational backgrounds. Liu, Chen, and Zhuang trained as architects for five years at Tongji University, which had originally been the Deutsche Medizinschule für Chinesen, a medical school for Chinese people founded by the German physician Erich Paulun in 1907. The architecture school itself was able to trace its lineage back to Shanghai's St. John's University, which was established by Huang Zuoshen, a former student of Walter Gropius. These twin pedigrees make Tongji particularly unique in the Chinese system for training architects, which has otherwise been dominated by Beaux Arts influences. The three Deshaus founders once recalled that even in the 1980s and 1990s when postmodernism was fashionable in architecture, the education at Tongji remained firmly based on modernist Bauhaus traditions. German was the primary foreign language for both Liu and Chen during their architectural studies.

The architectural training at Tongji no doubt profoundly influenced the subsequent works designed by Deshaus. Even though the firm would remind many of Bauhaus, the founders felt that Deshaus should first and foremost be understood as "having to do with the *Haus*," with a name adapted from the genitive form of the word *Haus* in German. This straightforward and humble explanation hints at a specific kind of attitude towards architecture: rather than merely being an expression of grandeur or superficiality, architecture has to return to its roots. These characteristics were undoubtedly present in Deshaus's early works; whether the Tri-house or the Dongguan Polytech building from the same period, the projects used a concise and clean formal language, clear volumetric relationships between the public and private, a rigorous and rational orthogonal grid, and architectural spaces that correspond to the logic of their functions, all of which are intentional demonstrations of modernist characteristics.

Even though the Chinese pictographic character 舍, corresponding to *Haus*, is used to approximate the pronunciation and meaning of Deshaus, its application nevertheless anticipates to some extent a change of course in the firm's later works. The buildings designed by Deshaus have always sought to blend traditions associated with China with the formal language of modernist architecture. That might be because the strategies adopted by the firm were often more roundabout and indirect, in contrast to those of many other Chinese architects back then, who had spent time studying or living in Europe or America and were thus faced with a sense of unease that comes from being in another cultural context. In the series of projects completed between 2003 and

From Structure to Language

2010 that included the Xiayu Kindergarten, Jiading New Town Kindergarten, and Qingpu Youth Center, Deshaus was confronted with the task of carefully situating new architecture into the existing historical and architectural context of the Jiangnan watertown region around Shanghai. The firm's response both rejected the kind of formal symbols that clearly expressed "Chineseness" while also choosing not to select materials and tectonics that might be more obviously suggestive of the visual forms for China. Instead, they insisted on the formal vocabulary of modernist architecture and did not exclude industrial materials such as corrugated perforated aluminum panels, screen-printed glass, and paints from the local area. Compared to the more direct strategies described above, Deshaus hoped to use something of a translational method to reinterpret the archetype of traditional spaces, and, moreover, to represent the perception and sensual experience of traditional spaces in an unfamiliar manner. As the architects wrote: "our works are intimately related to our understanding of the contextual culture of Jiangnan where we work; whether consciously or unconsciously, most of our architecture is like a small world unto itself [. . .] the archetype of this small world is the 'garden.'"

Operating according to the three concepts of "detach," "boundary," and "juxtaposition," Deshaus allowed Jiangnan to subtly feature in the Xiayu Kindergarten, for example, as a kind of spatial prototype and cultural form where the assorted courtyards and colorful volumes fall within clear boundaries; a further instance is the way that small-scale volumes form the passageways in Qingpu Youth Center. It is worth pointing out that the determination to create these "small self-sufficient worlds" comes from the architects applying critical thinking to their projects and showing a sensitivity to their own cultural backgrounds. This should also be understood as a response to the "new towns" of Jiading and Qingpu, which at the time were still largely blank slates. It is precisely the latter—the response to local conditions—that links tectonic traditions with the contemporary built environment.

If the early works produced by Deshaus 舍 could be said to be more about the tectonic traditions and cultural absorption of the Jiangnan region, then the attention paid more recently to official timber architecture since the Tang dynasty has gradually shifted the meaning of 舍 towards a more orthodox traditional Chinese architecture. It was while taking part in the 2018 exhibition *China House Vision* that Liu first proposed dismantling the logogram 舍 into its three component parts, namely 人 [ji], 屮 [cao], and 囗 [wei]. The installation piece 后舍 that was designed for the exhibition later became the spatial prototype for the Upper Cloister on Jinshan (Golden) Mountain. In an article from the same year called "Earthwork, trabeated system, and roof: three architectural elements of Foguang Temple from the perspective of *Sachlichkeit*," Liu tried to affirm just how fundamental and universal those three elements were to Chinese classical architecture by analyzing the composition of the logogram character 舍. This could be seen as an attempt to link Deshaus's architectural practice with a much grander, long-established tradition of construction. Just as Gottfried Semper similarly used the Primitive Hut as evidence for the four fundamental elements of architecture—wall, roof, hearth, and foundations—a reading that returns to fundamental elements in this manner weakens the specificity of culture in order to find the universality that transcends specific culture in special cases. In more recent works—the Tea House in Li Garden, Riverside Passage, and Upper Cloister—the spatial prototype from the three elements 人, 中, and 口 has formed an important theme for Deshaus.

Between 大舍 and Deshaus, the different names and meanings reveal an open approach to a range of practical situations and cultural contexts. From orthodox traditions of modernist architecture to contemplations about one's own culture, from the earlier interest in European architects from Spain and Switzerland to more recent exchanges with architects and structural engineers from Japan, Deshaus has continued to search for other sources of inspiration aside from the abstract tradition in modernism. On this basis, the firm has also rekindled a recognition of historic architecture. It is an openness that has allowed Deshaus to gradually develop its own architectural position under the influence of multiple sources.

"LIGHT" AND "MASS"
In May 2011, Liu published an article called "Light like a Bird: Case Studies from the Tables Designed by Junya Ishigami." It was in October of the same year that Liu began designing Long Museum, situated in the West Bund district of Shanghai. In reality, contemporary architecture, especially in Japan, has completed the erosion of modernism's robust structure by pursuing a kind of semi-transparent, light material effect. There seems to be an untraversable conceptual gap between the "lightness" of Junya Ishigami's table, Jürg Conzett's bridge, Toyo Ito's silver hut, and the "mass" of West Bund's Long Museum that is reminiscent of Hadrian's Villa and Rome. If the former could be said to have acquired a potential that is persistently iterative, being pushed to the extreme through a kind of technological drive that gives it an even more "contemporary" appearance, then the latter implies a permanence that transcends time. These two concepts mirror the parallel images of Deshaus's recent works. In Li Garden, Upper Cloister, and Riverside Passage, slender structural frames have created a kind of visual lightness while also achieving a large degree of fluidity between the interior and exterior. In the Spiral Gallery, Long Museum, and Taizhou Contemporary Art Museum, on the other hand, the use of concrete walls and the inherent directionality of the arch gives the works something of a spatial sensibility to mass, introversion, and

↑ Riverside Passage
↓ Upper Cloister on Jinshan (Golden) Mountain

From Structure to Language

solidity. This kind of binary interpretation is perhaps overly hasty as a judgment. A more careful reading would need to compare Long Museum with Toyo Ito's Tama Art University Library, which was the approach pursued by Liu in "Light like a Bird." Describing the technical detail of the delicate arch, Liu wrote: "Finally, the space formed by the thin arch is as tranquil as a sacred space, giving off a warm protective feeling while manifesting a natural and organic form. I think the 'thin' walls do have an effect on the uniqueness of this space. This 'thinness' achieved by the structure and construction technique have given this building an unprecedented contemporary experience. Although it is obviously different from any arched spaces of the past, it is also familiar." The unique nature of the space and the structural form of the thin arch are clearly intimately bound together. Ito has not dismantled the column and grid system of modernist architecture; it is rather the transformation of the relationship between column and beam that visually highlights the often-overlooked structure. In the Tama Art University Library, space remains the fluid space of modernist architecture, while structure has become a distinguishable entity. Long Museum formulates a kind of reversal of this relationship between space and structure. Even though the umbrella vault has often been understood as an iconic element in Long Museum, in reality, when visitors are in the exhibition galleries it is difficult to detect its visual existence. There is instead a perception of smoothly continuous arches gradually flowing from wall to ceiling, offering a sense of shelter and enclosure. So even though structure serves as the logic and means of constructing space, it is ultimately eroded by space. In comparison to the Tama Art University Library, space exists in the Long Museum West Bund as an even more powerful form. Thanks to the cantilever of the umbrella vault and the daylight coming from between the vaults, the structure has achieved a kind of "lightness" in perception while also realizing the heaviness of space.

Similarly, this kind of dialectical relationship between "lightness" and "heaviness," and between structure and space is also manifested in Riverside Passage. Here, thin columns with a sectional width of only 50 millimeters gracefully support a passageway on the long wall that was part of the original site. Structure naturally plays an important role, even framing a series of views towards the cityscape across Huangpu River; however, what ultimately stands out is the infinitely long space extending from one end of the wall to the other. Even though this "infinitely long" space has been defined as a "passage," it does not designate an end point. Rather, as the French critic Yehuda Safran commented when visiting Riverside Passage, one could almost pause there for a long while. The heaviness of the wall left from the industrial site and the fineness of metal structural members have formed a sharp visual contrast, while also complementing each other in offering a sense of intriguing ambiguity and balance, imparting a distinct sensibility of playfulness upon the architecture.

BEYOND (PRACTICING) ARCHITECTURE

If "lightness" and "heaviness" stem from Deshaus focusing on concepts concerned with architectural foundations such as structure and *Sachlichkeit* (objectivity) then the attention paid to art is another extended line of inquiry. Art museums and artists' studios feature prominently in the many projects completed by Deshaus in recent years. From the early unrealized design for artist Yue Minjun's studio to Long Museum West Bund, which is often seen as the work that best represents Deshaus, from the 80,000-ton art silo warehouse on Minsheng Wharf and the Modern Art Museum, both converted from industrial heritage sites, to the Qintai Art Museum, which is still under construction in Wuhan, Deshaus has continued to develop its understanding of architecture through the design process for this category of building. Beyond the architectural design of these art museums, Deshaus's participation in numerous art biennales and their collaborative works with artists are also not to be overlooked. One might claim these are the works that enabled Deshaus to push the boundaries of architecture, thereby venturing into the broader cultural sphere via contemporary art.

After a year spent setting up the firm, Deshaus exhibited the *Thatched Cottage* installation at the 2002 Shanghai Biennale, which ran under the motto of "Urban Creation." This extremely minimal spatial installation outlined a kind of "very thin, three-dimensional, linear modern agrarian rural" imagery. This was the piece that secured Deshaus's subsequent invitation to participate in the 2003 exhibition *Alors, la Chine?* at the Centre Pompidou in Paris. In this exhibition about Chinese contemporary art, Deshaus and seven other teams of participating architects recreated their own architectural works through collaborations with artists. Shanghai-based artists Xu Zhen and Yang Zhenzhong used video art to interpret their spatial experience in the Tri-house.

Throughout the following decade, Deshaus has continued to maintain close contacts with artists and curators. Contemporary art has inspired new breakthroughs on the fundamental tenets of architecture, which have been a major focus for Deshaus. The collaboration between Liu Yichun and artist Ding Yi on the Artron Art Center has opened up the discussion on ornament and facade. Using Ding Yi's iconic cross shape as a blueprint, the architect and the artist jointly designed forty-seven types of 100-mm-square ceramic tiles, which became the surface of the entire building, covering its interior and exterior walls as well as the floors. These tiles not only blurred the distinctions between the different structural elements but were also to be understood as a layer of skin that competes with the structure, even to the extent of completely hiding it. Accordingly, the Artron Art Center is more in tune with a highly visual and image-centric contemporary culture than other Deshaus works.

↑ *Tri-House*, video work by Deshaus, Xu Zhen, Yang Zhenzhong
ø *How It Flows On*, exhibition by Liu Yichun, Qiu Anxiong
↓ *Negative Sound Library*, art installation by Liu Yichun, Yin Yi

From Structure to Language

In the Blossom Pavilion, a 1+1 spatial art project created for the 2015 Shanghai Urban Space Art Season (SUSAS), Liu once more collaborated with an artist, this time transforming Zhan Wang's stainless steel rockery into a series of sliced rockery slabs that supported the pavilion. Even though it was the steel columns inside the sliced rockery that bore the structural load, the stainless steel, acting as the skin enclosing the columns, nevertheless became symbolic of the load-bearing element at the same time as it signified the collaboration with the artist. It is precisely contemporary art "stepping in" that has compelled the structure to transcend its nature as an object, thereby entering the abstract realm where symbol, meaning, and rhetoric subtly entangle, while also endowing the work with a more poetic appeal.

In recent years, such collaborations between Deshaus and various artists have emphasized overcoming the constraints of specified media. In two pieces, *Negative Sound Library* and *Art Museum*, which were made in collaboration with the sound artist Yin Yi, sound has become the other mode of perceiving space beyond vision. In the most recent exhibition *How it Flows On*, artist Qiu Anxiong and Liu Yichun have rebuilt a Riverside Passage at the APSMuseum in Pudong based on the simultaneity between the video and the projection. In addition to new opportunities for realizing design, these collaborations with artists have also brought perspectives from outside the discipline, thereby introducing a new discourse and fresh potential for addressing the issues of concern in the academic study of architecture.

UNPROGRAMMING AND THE AUTONOMY OF ARCHITECTURE

Since Plato and Aristotle, the theory of mimesis has always been fundamental to Western aesthetics and art theory. When nature is viewed in mimesis as the source of art, representation is achieved in poetry, painting, and sculpture by means of narration, delineation, and chiseling. The inherent functionality of architecture, on the other hand, means that it has always faced the dilemma of representation, so much so that Hegel placed architecture on the lowest rung in his philosophy of art. Art historian Rosalind Krauss, in her piece on Peter Eisenman and conceptual architecture, compared the logic of conceptual architecture with that of painting. If it could be said that classical painting emphasized the mimetic "image" presented on the canvas, whereby both the canvas and the paint were transparent and the viewer saw the painted "image," then modernist painting gradually began to recognize that the canvas is not transparent, that the painting is the paint, the canvas, and the strokes, and that there is no image being presented through the existence of all these materials. From the flickering, staggered strokes of Monet that gradually undid the three-dimensional attribute of pictorial space, returning to the two-dimensional surface of the canvas itself, to Lucio Fontana slashing open the canvas and finally acknowledging its materiality, the evolution of modernist painting can be read as a process of returning to the materiality of the canvas from its transparency. Art no longer derives its inherent value from re-presenting an image, just as Arnold Schöenberg's twelve-tone music turned composition into a kind of mathematical calculation or pure language that no longer exists in order to present a beautiful rhythm.

In a similar fashion, modernist architecture has tried to use the language of geometry and the abstractness of space to erase the baggage of mimesis in classical architecture, to liberate it from the complex ornamentation and strictures of the colonnade; however, architecture has never really returned to its roots. Modernist architecture's most famous slogan, "form follows function" has implied as much: as soon as architecture materializes, it needs to become what is from what it seems to be. As such, an art museum needs to adhere to notions about how an exhibition space is organized and how people circulate through that space in order to let its visitors feel that the space exists in accordance with the concept of an art museum. A kindergarten or school, similarly, needs to have a layout that fulfills the expectations of its users with respect to its specific contents. Under such circumstances, even though the space and structure have avoided the logic of mimesis, they are still caught up in the representation of functional and practical needs. The conceptual architecture represented by Eisenman is just such an attempt at establishing a system of pure architectural language, where the column and beam are elements in this pure architectural linguistic system rather than fulfilling their load-bearing function. Architecture, moreover, becomes a kind of spatial linguistic system with absolute autonomy in its concept, no longer constrained by specific functions.

Reading the Deshaus works against this backdrop is what makes them seem so unique. In the Long Museum, even though the curved concrete wall extending upwards could be used for hanging paintings or installations, and the exhibition space arranged in a windmill shape could also allow visitors to traverse freely, these uses come more from acquired, appended interpretations than from the innate qualities of the umbrella vaults and the space they create. Peter Eisenman once asked whether the architectural column was ultimately functional or symbolic as a structural element. A similar question could be posed about the Long Museum's umbrella vaults. Even if they have fulfilled their practical function, they have also *transcended* their function, and gained a kind of autonomous expression through their form and scale. In other words, in this case, the umbrella vault is no longer a structure that exists for a museum, existing instead for itself. This kind of phenomenological existence has even compelled Liu Yichun to mention in a lecture that when the concrete pour of the Long Museum's umbrella vaults was completed and its formwork removed: "I felt that the architecture could perhaps not be more beautiful than at that moment."

Similarly, even though the space shaped by rough concrete or slim steel columns have announced a certain kind of intention about their use at the Taizhou Contemporary Art Museum, Riverside Passage, and Upper Cloister on Jinshan (Golden) Mountain, they could also be something else as well. Actually, before Taizhou Contemporary Art Museum officially opened, its unfinished space indeed resembled a natural theater, where some people meandered, others held parties or took wedding photographs, and some artists even used it as a creative space. These architectures invited people to enter and feel their spaces, even offering a free imagining of their uses rather than observing the uses designated for them. It is precisely in this sense that architecture is no longer the medium for realizing other purposes but instead finally becomes an existence for the thing itself. This kind of architecture no doubt draws us to think of Martin Heidegger's view of "the thing," which has influenced Liu and Chen profoundly. It perhaps explains too why Liu has often referenced a sentence from Jacques Derrida, which Eisenman also quotes in his introduction to the English translation of Aldo Rossi's *The Architecture of the City*: "...the relief and design of structures appears more clearly when content, which is the living energy of meaning, is neutralized, somewhat like the architecture of an uninhabited or deserted city, reduced to its skeleton by some catastrophe of nature or art. A city no longer inhabited, not simply left behind, but haunted by meaning and culture, this state of being haunted, which keeps the city from returning to nature, is perhaps the general mode of the presence or absence of the thing itself in pure language..."

CONCLUSION
Set against a background of rapid developments in contemporary China, with architectural designs that are driven by the magnitude of these developments, and given the nature of architecture as a profession that incorporates various disciplines such as engineering, culture, art, and engineering design, it has become easier to resolve the problems of specific functions, although factors that are more critical and culturally aware at the core of disciplinary autonomy do seem difficult to address. The works of Deshaus are rare amongst Chinese contemporary architects in attempting to return architecture to the ontological level of its language by means of "unprogramming." The philosophy of phenomenology, which originated in Germany and was an early influence for Liu and Chen, advocated discarding all additives and defining and confronting the essence of things. From the perspective of contemporary conceptual

↑ Plain concrete space, Taizhou Contemporary Art Museum

art and architecture, the dissolution of existing professional frameworks in the discipline and the erosion of existing disciplinary systems are largely reflected in their writings as well. Their texts contain the dialectical thinking of phenomenology and seek the origins of concepts, yet without eschewing the poetic depictions of literary affinity.

The architecture designed by Liu and Chen is just like their texts, for they create buildings from the rationality of structure and the poetry of space while also trying to establish an architectural system that possesses pure linguistic meaning and transcends functionality.

Whether starting the design from the structure, or focusing on the space, Deshaus's architectural and artistic works ultimately give birth to a form of pure language. Architecture is thus also able to extricate itself from the typological definition of the specific art museum, school, or kindergarten to become a kind of abstract architecture with a capital A. If it could be said to have a function, then the ways in which people might linger, look around, relax, and also resonate emotionally in the space are the most authentic and valuable assets of architecture. This seems to be precisely what Deshaus is meticulously pursuing—but it is also the reason that their works stand out amidst the mass of architectural practice from contemporary China.

Li Shiqiao

THE RETURN OF THE LITERATI

Atelier Deshaus, along with other architectural practices in China such as Feichang Jianzhu (Yung Ho Chang), Jiakun Architects (Liu Jiakun), Li Xiaodong Atelier (Li Xiaodong), Amateur Architecture Studio (Wang Shu and Lu Wenyu), and Standardarchitecture (Zhang Ke), presents us with something more than captivating architecture. They represent what may be described as the return of the literati (translations of the terms *shi* and *wenren*). The idea of the architect is understandably constructed around cultural archetypes of persons; mainstream versions of the idea of the architect seem to have been modeled around several primary archetypes rooted in the European cultural context: the hero, the saint, the avant-garde, and the expert, each propelling architecture in a specific direction. The hero descends from Greek mythology as an offspring of gods and mortals, living among humans and possessing comprehensive physical and intellectual abilities; athlete, Papal secretary, poet, artist, architect, and philosopher Leon Battista Alberti (1404–1472) exemplifies the cultivation of this personality so appealing to the European Renaissance. Following the fall of the Roman Empire, the prestige of the saint soared along with the rise of the Christian faith; mystic Eastern meditation, the Hebrew tradition of the sacred book, and the office of the priesthood all created a religious context in which the individual engaged in a perpetual moral struggle against temptation gained tremendous moral and aesthetic status. Michelangelo (1475–1564) comes close to this mode of being with his tormented yet supremely skillfully executed poems, paintings, sculptures, and buildings. The avant-garde accompanied the rise of modernity, with a tenacious and fearless adherence to convention-defying rational thought, research, and artistic creations that startle and delight. Le Corbusier (1887–1965), with all his hyperbole and the bold spatial constructs of an avant-garde architect, announced new moral and aesthetic futures of modernity in architecture. The expert, despite their prudence, has become an important archetype for our age; as a consequence of the specialization that was already apparent in the Humboldtian model of the University of Berlin in the nineteenth century, the expert has perhaps become the most valuable person in ensuring the fruitful development of science and technology in the service of the endless accumulation of capital, which forms the basis of our current capitalist and consumerist world-system. Norman Foster (1935–) leads the expert architects in providing stunning and sophisticated structures of steel, glass, and concrete that deliver elegant solutions to problems of convenience and hygiene, with the resulting architecture filled with air, light, and the luxury of spaciousness in an age of efficiency. Today, architects navigate around these archetypes as they position their practices and conceive designs to find a firm ground in professional practice.

THE FALL AND RISE OF THE LITERATI

Despite China's introduction of the European- and American-style architectural profession in the twentieth century, these cultural archetypes do not seem to reproduce well in China without the deeper European traditions. China's traditional exemplary persons are derived largely from two sets of categories: the first is the scholar *(shi)*, peasant farmer *(nong)*, artisan *(gong)*, and merchant *(shang)* characterization, which also embodied an inherent value hierarchy for each type of person that differs considerably from the European model. The second set is a tripartite construct of the powerful official *(guan)*, the courageous soldier *(jiang)*, and the wise scholar-literati *(wenren)*. Overall, it was these scholar-literati who occupied the center of cultural values; the scholar-literati maintained the capacity of balancing the thoughtful, the spiritual, the courageous, and the knowledgeable in one single life form. The scholar-literati figure is arguably the most admired person in China. Their ability to delight an audience with elegant poems interlaced with erudite literary references and their carefully curated gardens with endless figurations exert a powerful grip on China's cultural imagination. Chinese culture celebrates its numerous accomplished scholar-literati, who are intellectually constituted to be fundamentally differently from the hero, the saint, the avant-garde, and the expert: the courageous Qu Yuan (340–278 BCE), the delightful Li Bai (701–762), the patriotic Du Fu (712–770), and the candid Bai Juyi (772–846), and so on. Twentieth-century literary giants such as Lu Xun (1881–1936), Zhu Ziqing (1898–1948), Ba Jin (1904–2005), Ding Ling (1904–1986), and Zhang Ailing (1920–1995), among many others, keep the notion of the literati alive in the imagination of contemporary China.

For all the high cultural value vested in Chinese society, the literati had a path to political power by becoming what was known in the traditional context as a scholar-official *(shidafu)*. The means of securing scholar-officialdom in the imperial court was the civil service examination, which was conducted from around the seventh century until its abolition in 1905. The most prestigious degree from this set of demanding examinations was that of "presented scholar" (*jinshi*), which ensured a well-compensated and respected career in the imperial administration. This system was once greatly admired by European Enlightenment thinkers such as Voltaire and Leibniz, who wished to separate talent and bureaucracy from blood inheritance. China's most iconic love tales such as the thirteenth-century Story of the Western Wing *(Xixiang Ji)* and the sixteenth-century Peony Pavilion *(Mudan Ting)* are associated with the progress of young aspiring scholars—at the center of love stories—as they take part in civil service examinations and exhibit the talent and potential for scholar-officialdom. China's most stunningly beautiful gardens were constructed by literati-officials, forming a key spatial manifestation of the extraordinary institution of scholar-officialdom.

The abolition of the civil service examination system in 1905 was perhaps the strongest indication that China had lost confidence in its traditional institutions when global geopolitical developments had placed the country under immense stress in the preceding half century. Like all aspects of Chinese cultural life, the civil service examination system became deeply conventionalized in the Qing dynasty (1644–1911), China's last imperial dynasty under the Manchu lineage. During the same period, the world witnessed the dramatic rise of Europe as a result of scientific, agricultural, and industrial transformations, leading to unprecedented economic advancement and global expansion. The first Opium War (1839–1842) gave European countries access to China's trade, which was crucial to the establishment of the global trading system that the European bourgeoisie so desired. Traditional institutions crumbled in China one after the other, even though most Chinese intellectuals wished to sustain the country's traditional culture. Liang Qichao's reformism brought extensive European ideas to help reframe Confucianism for imperial reforms. Sun Yat-sen's republicanism (1912–1949) and Mao's socialism (1949–) were more radically mapped for China onto European political ideals and government models. The shock to the literati in China was perhaps most vividly captured in the novels and life of Lu Xun, whose own adaptation as a traditional scholar to China's new century resulted in a literati-hero and a literati-avant-garde hybrid.

The transformation of the literati was even greater under Mao; they were reformulated as the "knowledgeable members" (*zhishi fenzi*) of society, and became a target for reform and violence during the radical Cultural Revolution (1966–1976) for being too out of touch with Chinese culture, as narrowly defined by peasant folk culture. Both the story of the twelfth-century construction manual called *Yingzao Fashi*, and the lives of the Chinese architect couple Liang Sicheng (1901–1972) and Lin Huiyin (1904–1955), who were both University of Pennsylvania graduates, are examples of what this radical transformation of China's literati meant for architecture. From the ashes of the Cultural Revolution, it was the European and American archetypes of the hero, the saint, the avant-garde, and the expert that initially captured the imagination of the Chinese youth in the 1980s, the generation that is now shaping China's architecture. It has taken forty years for China's architects to reimagine themselves as the descendants of the literati, having internalized the demands of a contemporary architectural practice and the deep and often violent transformation of the Chinese literati in the twentieth century. Despite being born into the wasteland of the Cultural Revolution and spellbound by European and American architecture, against all the odds they pursued the Chinese architectural tradition in a contemporary context. They have made a conscious and determined return to the tradition of the Chinese literati.

LIU YICHUN AND THE NEW LITERATI

Born in 1969 at the height of the Cultural Revolution, Liu Yichun embodies this return to the literati in the most exciting ways, amidst what is perhaps the most profound transformation ever in Chinese architecture. While studying architecture at Tongji University, Liu was mesmerized by European and American architecture and culture. He was a lover of rock 'n' roll and world literature, studied German as a second language, and designed modernist projects for his studio assignments at a time when other Chinese schools were teaching Beaux-Arts-style renderings. Shortly after graduation, Liu got together with Zhuang Shen and Chen Yifeng in 2001 to found Atelier Deshaus, choosing a German-sounding name for their company. The firm's early work, the Tri-house (2003), was unapologetically modernist, defiantly holding its own among the pseudo European-style houses that surrounded the Tri-house and were extremely popular at the time.

However, the Chinese name of their firm, Da She (meaning the "great habitat" or "big house"), has an entirely different set of cultural references. The Chinese character for "habitat" *(she)* comprises the figures of a roof, a column bracket set, and a foundation. Liu's father, Liu Shitong, had never received a normal university education because he belonged to the Cultural Revolution's "wasted generation" who went to rural villages to toil with the peasants instead of attending college; Mao believed that this would change their moral and aesthetic values for good. Working in an umbrella factory and as a teacher of Chinese in a high school, Liu Shitong was passionate about poetry and literature; he became—and remained—friends with many talented literary figures while they were in the countryside. He published a collection of poems (partly supported with the money from Liu Yichun's first independent job) as well as novels and literary writing. Moreover, he subscribed to the most important literary journals in China, where most creative Chinese literature debuted after the Cultural Revolution, and also built up a library of great literary works. Liu Yichun grew up among these friendships, books, and journals.

Like many Chinese children, Liu Yichun was instructed by his father to recite Tang poetry, which has strict formal requirements, but he actually prefers the freer forms of Song verse. Every aspect of his father's love for literature exerted an incremental and deep influence on Liu Yichun, forming the background for his later encounter with world literature: *The Sorrows of Young Werther* by Goethe, *The Scarlet Letter* by Hawthorne, *Wuthering Heights* by Brontë, *The Red and the Black* by Stendhal, *Madame Bovary* by Flaubert, *Resurrection* and *Anna Karenina* by Tolstoy. One of his personal favorites is *The World of Yesterday* by Zweig. Having been banned for a decade, these literary classics generated tremendous excitement among China's youth in the 1980s, even though they were read in the form of Chinese translations. It is important to understand this entirely unique intellectual situation as forming a key aspect of the establishment of China's new literati. If the arrival of world literature in post-Cultural Revolution China was sudden and dramatic, the return of the traditional literati was gradual yet profound.

Among the first to gain international recognition were those who studied in Europe and America as soon as the opportunity came their way. Yung Ho Chang, who had studied at Ball State University and UC Berkeley, established Feichang Jianzhu as the first private architectural practice in China following the Cultural Revolution, thereby giving the world a foretaste of what the new literati could look like. An extraordinary talented conceptual thinker and designer, Chang's architectural radicalism is interwoven with delightful literary skills (both in English and Chinese) and self-effacing humor, paralleling some of the distinctive traits of the traditional literati character. It is perhaps this unique combination that schools of architecture outside China found so appealing: Chang held the Kenzo Tange Chair at Harvard Graduate School of Design and the Eliel Saarinen Chair at University of Michigan, and served as head of the Department of Architecture at MIT. Li Xiaodong studied at Tsinghua University and TU Delft, winning the Aga Khan Award in 2010 with his stunning projects in rural China, which are often completed on a charitable basis; his designs are a critical yet—in seeking idyllic isolation—profoundly Chinese response both to China's mass production of bland architecture and to the instrumental understanding of space in Europe and America. Zhang Ke, another Tsinghua graduate who studied at the Harvard Graduate School of Design, won the Aga Khan Award in 2016 and the Alvar Aalto Medal in 2017 with designs that are uniquely sensitive to materials, spaces, and the histories of locations in Tibet and Beijing; although a feature common to many great works of architecture worldwide, Zheng Ke's rendition of localities and materials have a distinct echo of China's literati sensibilities.

The skills with which these architects, and many others, negotiated their works on the global scene are remarkable, but more significant was the parallel emergence of architects within China itself. More steeped in China's ancient tradition and more heavily invested in its critical renewal, these architects—who typically have fewer foreign language skills and less experience of living abroad—had to invent more critical tools in more distinctive ways. Being so deeply rooted in Chinese culture was long regarded as a disadvantage, but now it is clearly viewed as an immense strength and a testament to their originality. Writer and architect Liu Jiakun is an extraordinary example of how creative practice takes shape in contemporary China; he sees his architecture as being neither beginnings nor ends, but rather efficacious interventions of continuous and fluid material and spatial continuities. "I don't seek an ideal life and environment," says Liu, highlighting one of the most distinctively productive intellectual features in China (both in Daoism and Confucianism): namely the absence of a notion of "being" or "becoming." China's new literati focused on the cultural forms that emerged in the period between the eighth and sixteenth centuries, when the dynasties of the Tang, the Song, and the Ming gave rise to a tremendous legacy of poetry, literature, painting, and gardens. The region with the best and most abundant examples of literati cultural life was Jiangnan (literally meaning "south of the river," this is the area covered more or less by the modern-day provinces of Jiangsu and Zhejiang), on account of its rich waterways, mild climate, traditional wealth, and highly cultivated intellectual setting. Here we find literati gardens as perhaps the most powerful demonstration of literati life in Jiangnan, posing as a provocative parallel to European and American theories and practices. One of the key distressing realities in China facing this generation of architects is the rapid construction of large amounts of mediocre buildings and urban areas; these are neither interesting as new (European and American inspired) architecture, nor traditional Chinese in any perceivable sense. Wang Shu's and Lu Wenyu's return to the traditional sensibility of poetic interactions with nature is pitched against the era of mass mediocrity; as Dean of the School of Architecture at the China Academy of Art, Wang Shu gathered a group of talented young architects and researchers who were pushing the boundaries of Chinese architecture in the context of a new century. Many others returned in the same way; for instance, Dong Yugan of Peking University, Tong Ming of Tongji University, and Ge Ming of Southeast University established an academic platform, the "And Series," to reframe contemporary architectural theory and practice through Chinese categories of thought. The first volume in the And Series was *Garden and Architecture* (2009), a book that deliberately deviated from the normative historical studies of Chinese gardens by introducing a strong theoretical focus, an intention underlined by the inclusion of translated writings by scholars of Chinese philosophy Roger Ames and David Hall, theorist of art Rosalind Krauss, and landscape architect James Corner. The authors were striving not merely to reproduce traditional Chinese architecture but to place and modify it in a critical context of European and American architectural theories and practices.

The development of this search for a Chinese literati architecture became more apparent with the publication of the three volumes in the Arcadia Series between 2014 and 2018, inspired by a Ming-dynasty reference to a "non-existent garden." Published by Tongji University Press and edited by Jin Qiuye and Wang Xin, these beautiful volumes explore the relationship between painting and architecture, illusion and reality, and contemplation and construction in the Chinese intellectual context. Unlike the 2009 And Series, these books are more focused on the Chinese literati and its environmental designs, filled with in-depth knowledge of the techniques of assembling rocks for gardens and inventions of terms that attempt to capture the Chinese spatial order and the poetic experience. The volumes feature Dong Yugan's Red Brick Museum in Beijing (2014), Li Xinggang's Jixi Museum (2013), and Ge Ming's Wei Garden (2015), among many other projects, which brought a material reality to what this return of the Chinese literati could mean for a new kind of Chinese architecture.

In 2017, Wang Shu and Wang Xin crucially conceptualized an extraordinary exhibition at the Folk Art Museum of the China Academy of Art that was both wonderfully inventive and originally Chinese. Organized around five "scenes"—spatializing the acts of seeing far, sleeping with water, living in painting, accommodating one's knees in a corner, and drinking tea at home to reflect travel—with their corresponding literati practices, Wang Shu and Wang Xin injected immense vitality and relevance into the cultural life of the Chinese literati. In naming delightful poetic experiences related to the Chinese spatial order—much like a traditional literati would have done—Wang Xin laid out unique spaces, at once richly Chinese and accessibly contemporary. Unlike scholars in imperial China, this generation of Chinese architects are far more informed and open-minded towards European and American influences; the tumultuous twentieth century removed some of the fears of modifying Chinese traditions for the future.

Liu Yichun actively took part in many of these events with great fascination. Among this group of architects in China, Liu is perhaps the least concerned with referring to material forms of traditional China, and the most motivated by an inherent Chinese spatial order that is thing-based and fluid at the same time, the result of a poetic invention that takes the distinctive features of buildings, materials, and locations into account. It is, however, not a methodology in the sense of the principles of tectonics or theoretical expositions. The combination of Liu Yichun's love for contemporary materials and his passion for Chinese design makes his architecture more intriguing than the direct material references in the works of many other Chinese architects. Atelier Deshaus's first independent project in 2005, the Xiayu Kindergarten in Shanghai, was already the result of an intense investigation into the spatial order of the garden of the Master of the Nets (Wangshi Yuan) in Suzhou. Xiayu Kindergarten was located in Shanghai's Qingpu District, one of many new towns that Shanghai had started building in the early 2000s as part of its ambitious urban expansion. Unlike many other new towns where exotic European styles were highly desirable (such as Thames Town), the Qingpu District was imagined as a Jiangnan-style new town. Xiayu Kindergarten, as well as several other early projects such as Jishan Base in Jiangsu Software Park (2008) and Qingpu Youth Center (2012), took the task of creating a new Jiangnan style to heart.

ARCHITECTURE AS POETIC INVOCATION (SHIYI)

This fluid judgment in the establishment of a Chinese spatial order is not mysterious for anyone who has some degree of familiarity with both the Chinese writing system and how that system orders the world through figuration, as I attempted to describe in *Understanding the Chinese City* (2014). The key here is the creation of the poetic experience in ordering the world as the moral and aesthetic experience anchoring human life. This experience should not be alienated by instrumentality (Heidegger, perhaps influenced by Chinese philosophy, pursued a path in this direction deep into European philosophy). The invocation of the Master of the Nets garden in the first design undertaken by Atelier Deshaus is a reminder that the poetic experience in China is quite averse to instrumental efficacy, which has been a key character of the European culture *(deus ex machina)*. There is neither god nor machine (in all its varieties in mechanization, linguistic structure, and data analytics); instead, we live with a distribution of things and figures. Although the site of the Master of the Nets garden can be dated back to the twelfth century, its current form was built in the late eighteenth century. It is small (1.3 acres), yet skillfully arranged through detours and spatial depth in spite of its size, exemplifying the effectiveness of garden design. The Master of the Nets is a curatorial endeavor that aims to assemble "thing-truths" with exceptional value and rarity while establishing the prestige and status of the scholar-official through an astonishing display of erudition, poetic invention, and value. We have no other category for framing it today apart from "architecture" or "landscape," but it is much more than these: It is an entirely different way of relating to the world, for which Indo-European civilization has no real precedent. At the heart of the Master of the Nets—and the numerous other gardens in Jiangnan and their derivatives in other parts of China—is a conviction that the unit of relating to the world is the thing and its figure, rather than the instrumentality of its molecular structures. The school of thought known as Mohism, which was advocated by Mozi (470–391 BCE), pursued what could have become Chinese instrumentality through science and logic, but gradually gave way to Daoism and Confucianism. This conceptual divide cannot be more fundamental. The molecular structural view of the world assumes no fixed figures in the final instance, perceiving the world as comprising much smaller units that are made up of fixed structures: Plato's two primary number series, five solids, and the contemporary framing through DNA embody this understanding. The figurative view of the world positions itself against the notion that the whole is accountable through the sum of its parts (if indeed parts are identifiable); it is in the unit of the thing that meaning is located. Visually, this meaning unit is embodied in the "figure" of the thing; what holds all the figures and meanings together is a fluid and ceaselessly transforming balance. The Master of the Nets works with these figures rather than with a numerical or tectonic system to establish a meaningful environmental modification. It creates the substance of poetic experience that the new Chinese literati were yearning for.

↑ Plan, Master of the Nets garden

Among all cultural artifacts in China, it is the Chinese writing system that provides the firmest grounding for this fluid judgment in ordering the world as something that leads to a poetic experience. In fact, it is exceedingly difficult to reproduce outside the Chinese writing system. Perhaps it also explains the extraordinary originality of the new literati, who relied primarily on the Chinese language. Instead of investing in an abstract alphabetic system that notates sounds, the Chinese writing system uses units of visual images. Although many of them do not have their origins in the images of things, and some of the components do have a phonetic function, the central feature of the writing system is to allow a web of meanings to be constructed at the level of the thing or its equivalent. Reading the reflective writings of Chinese architects, one is constantly informed of the decisive influences from the origins, meanings, and shapes of these Chinese characters. They anchor the notion of a Chinese spatial order, which is invariably both literary and material. One of the most neglected components in the study of Chinese gardens is the density and meaning of Chinese characters (tablets, couplets, calligraphy), without which the poetic experience cannot be established. This is perhaps why Heidegger's endeavor to break away from the instrumentality of European thought is profoundly and frustratingly undermined by the instrumentality of the alphabetic language he still exclusively relied on. François Jullien's strategy of establishing a temporary detour from that same instrumentality via the Chinese language—which is crucial to an understanding of divergence *(écart)* in cultures—is far more successful than Heidegger's.

THE FOUR GUIDING CHARACTER-PRINCIPLES OF ATELIER DESHAUS
Liu Yichun is understandably anxious about the English translation of four Chinese characters that seem to encapsulate the fundamental design principles of Atelier Deshaus: *yin* (seizing productive contextual forces), *jie* (leveraging the advantageousness of the surroundings), *ti* (formal states of judicious existence), and *yi* (being appropriately situated). There is much at stake here; it concerns not just the key design strategies of an architectural design firm but also the efficacy of Chinese culture, since these four characters are taken from a gardening handbook entitled *The Craft of Gardens (Yuan Ye)* written by Ji Cheng between 1631 and 1634 in the late Ming dynasty when garden building was at its zenith. Atelier Deshaus operates almost entirely without formal references to traditional Chinese architecture; but this only highlights the importance of understanding these four principles without which their works can easily be misplaced in misleading cultural contexts. Atelier Deshaus's use of concrete, steel, glass, and mirror has a cultural function that must not get lost in translation.

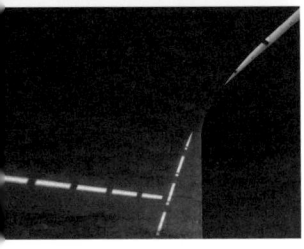

In 2014, the stunningly beautiful Long Museum in Shanghai brought Atelier Deshaus to the world's attention on account of its extraordinary spaces, light, and materiality. Indeed, the museum has proven so inspiring to curators and artists around the globe (Olafur Eliasson, to take just one example) that they have produced site-specific works to be situated in the concrete surfaces and interlocking spaces instead of the generic white backgrounds and boxes of most art museums. The architecture has two other layers: Lurking behind the building is the remains of an old coal dock that handled the logistics of coal from the western provinces, and there also are the foundations of a project for a tourist information center. This is the perfect point for introducing the first two character-principles (*yin* and *jie*) into our understanding of this work, and weighing this against the obvious connection with the European notion of the ruin.

The key Chinese conception here is the trace, not the ruin. Trace *(ji)* is ubiquitous in Chinese thought and practice as a way of establishing a conception of time. Although all cultures share the fact of time's passing, the intellectual conceptions of what time actually is can differ fundamentally. The traditional Chinese sense of time, which is embedded in the word "trace," is not constructed through clear categories of the past in terms of antiquity, historical periods, or future states. Karl Jasper coined the notion of "axial age": a time when the major world civilizations took on their defining characters from the eighth to the third century BCE, when, he observed, only Confucianism and Daoism did not have a clear order of the past. Rather than being conceived as having passed, time in the Chinese context was imagined as remaining present through traces. Ancient Greek, Persian, and Indian religions all had distinctive concepts of past orders, which is important to maintain the significance of ruins. As I have argued in "Memory without Location" (a chapter in my book *Understanding the Chinese City*), in Greek culture the character of memory was deeply associated with locations, and Christianity transformed the Greek location-based memory strategy into one that is embedded in the ruin of the body of Christ. The concept of the relic provided the basis for pilgrimages, and with this came the rise of medieval European cities. Ruins do not seem to have made sense in traditional Chinese cultural practice if they are not there as traces; they only brought imperfections to the fore. The intellectual discourse of trace in Chinese architecture is still at its early stages, and inevitably the existing grid of the parking basement and the old structures of the coal dock funnels are often framed by architectural writers as ruins, invoking the long established theory and practice that involved the ruins of past orders. Here, while the notion of the ruin is interesting, it is also deeply misleading. It is merging the past and present with traces of time *(henji)* that ultimately gave rise to the poetic experience of the Long Museum.

↑ Bridge for unloading coal
↓ Plain concrete space

The Long Museum is followed by a series of projects that leveraged similar dynamics: the 2016 Modern Art Museum, the 2017 Renovation and Reuse of the 80,000-ton Silos, and the 2019 Riverside Passage. All of them are located along the major river flowing through Shanghai, the Huangpu, where many sites marking Shanghai's industrial past await development. In 2010, Shanghai hosted the World Expo at the southern end of the industrial sites, and Yu Kongjian's Turenscape designed the environment-healing Houtan Park in the same year. What Atelier Deshaus projects demonstrate, time and again, is Liu Yichun's strategy of "seizing productive contextual forces" *(yin)*, and "leveraging the advantageousness of the surroundings" *(jie)*. The opportunities clearly varied considerably; at the Long Museum, the need to work with the existing column grid and the shape of the loading bridge for coal hoppers inspired the concrete "vault umbrellas" that set the tone for the entire design. At the Modern Art Museum, the key concept came from its Chinese name *yicang* ("art storage"), referring to the "coal storage" facility *(meicang)* that preceded the art museum. The structural idea was central to the success of this design: the old coal storage is completely swathed in a layer of new spaces that are suspended from the existing structure of the coal storage, creating a rich set of spatial interests. The traces of Shanghai's industrial past have been brought back to life—not encased as ruins—in an attempt to give Shanghai's art a contemporary presence. Very differently conceived, the renovation of the 80,000-ton silos built just over twenty years ago along the industrial sites of Huangpu River. In this case the design seized the potential of the silos' imposing monumentality. Unintentionally iconic, these silos are the very essence of the contextual force. Liu Yichun takes a much lighter approach here, perceptively realizing that while the coal storage facility needed to mobilize a dramatic design to create interest, the silos only required minimal modifications. The addition of the main vertical circulation through a set of escalators along Huangpu River was the minimum possible intervention with a transformative capacity, enabling the use of the lower and upper levels—the grain silos are 48 meters high—as exhibition spaces. The Riverside Passage was a project to renovate the open-air coal storage for a gas factory that featured a rare 90-meter-long concrete wall on a concrete platform next to Huangpu River. Deeply moved by the aesthetic potential of this simple wall, Liu Yichun revived it with a project he called *Bian Yuan* or "edge garden," which is a homonym invoking the characters for "margin," namely *bianyuan*. The wall is its own contextual force, which Liu Yichun, as a literatus, seizes in order to transform it into a linear garden incorporating an arena for skateboarding and roller skating (two very popular activities just beyond the plaza of the Long Museum). All these traces that have been brought back to life to construct a sense of time and its passing demonstrate the efficacy of *yin* and *jie* as concepts that are so fundamental to the works of Atelier Deshaus.

↑ The Modern Art Museum under construction
↓ Existing wall and wild trees, Riverside Passage

No less important is Liu Yichun's exploration of the judicious states of architecture *(ti)*: Chinese architecture has not traditionally invested in the notion of origins, thus the "primitive hut" narrative does not seem to have sufficient cultural cachet, in sharp contrast to the intense speculations on origins in the European cultural and intellectual context. Since Vitruvius, treatises and theories of architecture have always been concerned with tracing mythical and technical origins, whether this is Solomon's Temple, the primitive hut, or the ideal villa (Villa Rotunda, Chiswick House, Villa Savoye, Barcelona Pavilion, etc.). These histories and theories constitute an intellectual double of the ruin; if the ruin highlights the impossibility that perfection once existed, the ideal villa stubbornly reasserts its tentative viability. To some extent, European epistemology is also characterized by seeking the origins of things, a goal of knowledge that is very different from the Chinese focus on the propensity of things. Liu Yichun's House ATO in 2018, designed for a housing exhibition initiated by the Japanese architect Kenya Hara, exemplifies this divergence. Here, the fundamental issues are centered on the generality of the habitat *(she)*—the roof, the column, the foundations—which had already been explored in his 2016 Tea House in Li Garden and the 2015 office space for Atelier Deshaus itself. At House ATO, figuration is in full force; the visual logic of the character *she* becomes the first basis for the architecture; House ATO—the three Roman letters that most closely resemble the shapes of the roof, column, and foundations in the Chinese character *she*—is Liu Yichun's boldest attempt at bridging the swamp of translation. Typology vanishes here, but then again, traditional Chinese architecture never embraced typology. Instead, House ATO is turned into the fundamental unit of the space for life, be it a house, a meeting room, a shop, a temple, a garden. The building itself becomes almost like something painted by a brush; all the structural and constructional forms are deliberately designed away. It is a building that is truly "like painting" *(ruhua)*, a key conception of the poetic experience emerging from the skills of the literati.

Taizhou Contemporary Art Museum, which was completed in 2019, is a material expression of Liu Yichun's concern that architecture be appropriately situated *(yi)*. Popularized as *feng shui*, the appropriate situation has been a long-cherished principle of the literati, as Ji Cheng's 1631 *The Craft of Gardens* demonstrates. Both a Daoist principle and a Confucianist social canon, being appropriately situated is also a clear design strategy. Suzhou gardens are often masterful examples of appropriate situations; perhaps the dense urban context and the relatively small sizes of these gardens made it particularly profitable to maximize the advantages of the site's conditions. Taizhou Contemporary Art Museum is a building created by the conditions of the site. The key design strategy was to establish clear visual contact with Feng Mountain (which is the

↑ Upper Cloister under construction
↓ Plain concrete space, Taizhou Contemporary Art Museum

dominant contextual feature) by ingeniously manipulating the height of each of the eight exhibition rooms. Feng Mountain appears as "paintings" in different frames as one moves from space to space (the *ruhua* or "painting-like" quality). In Qintai Art Museum (2021), Liu Yichun returns to the rockery of the Chinese literati garden, just as Wang Shu and Wang Xin had done so brilliantly, to design "cavities" (exhibition rooms) and "mountaintops" (rooftop walkways), each offering winding paths and varying views to invoke a deep poetic experience through their references to China's architectural traditions.

FIGURATIVE REFLEXIVITY
One of the most problematic character traits of the traditional Chinese literati is their disposition to disengage with polity; their preferred existence, if out of favor at the imperial court, was some form of self-imposed isolation. The diversity of literati cultivation was generally manifested as "schools" *(pai)*, which was anchored by a form of piety akin to the Confucianist loyalty to the family. The kind of public criticism as a profession that was practiced in the early eighteenth-century London journals *The Tatler* and *The Spectator* (founded by Richard Steele and Joseph Addison, with Jonathan Swift a notable contributor) has never been a feature of traditional Chinese intellectual life. Instead, immense prestige was associated exclusively with the schools. So is there room for criticality in the life of the Chinese literati? The cultural revolutions in China following the Opium Wars did give rise to this possibility; Lu Xun was one of the twentieth-century Chinese intellectuals who embodied a version of the literati combined with the European model of the cultural avant-garde. It was this reflexivity that reemerged after the Cultural Revolution, most prominently in literature and art.

The expression "figurative reflexivity" may be appropriate to describe this relatively recent yet tremendously important intellectual development in China. If, in spirit, this figurative reflexivity attempts to attain a similar level of self-criticality as the European "structural reflexivity," it is, however, largely embedded in the cultural context of the Chinese literati. First, it tends to be a practice rather than a theory, and second, it is about figuration rather than about structure. Zhan Wang (1962–), who is part of a generation of extraordinarily talented artists such as Xu Bing, Ai Weiwei, and Qiu Zhijie, worked with a distinctively Chinese approach of refiguring. Instead of dismantling the structure of an artifact and recreating new structures as in the works of Monet and Picasso, these artists strove to maintain the integrity of the figure while placing them in critically challenging new contexts. Xu Bing, in his powerful *Book from the Sky* (1987–1991), used a set of about 3,000 fictitious "Chinese characters" he invented to recreate traditional forms of literary volumes and scrolls with established book-making techniques, invoking enormous anxiety among China's intellectuals and politicians who sensed an existential crisis of Chinese culture in his art. This work, in a fundamental way, brings critical attention to the foundational importance of the Chinese writing system for Chinese civilization. Qiu Zhijie's *Writing the "Orchid Pavilion Preface" One Thousand Times* (1990–1995) reenacted some aspects of the literati's training through copying classics; however, here the copying was all carried out on the same piece of paper so that the end result is illegible blackness. Zhan Wang's *Artificial Rock* series (1995–) presented stainless-steel sculptures that had been meticulously handcrafted to reproduce the exquisite shapes of the rockery in literati gardens, thereby putting a reflective shine on a cultural icon, as if to extract reflexivity out of the viewer. His *Urban Landscape* series (2003–2005) recreated urban scenes by using polished stainless-steel kitchen utensils, bringing the hygienic and instrumental urban reality to a dramatic display. All these incredibly powerful and creative works relied on the critical dislocation of things and figures; in important ways, they demonstrated a figurative reflexivity that is different from the European and American practice of identifying and disassembling structures, from Impressionism through to Cubism.

Liu Yichun has been collaborating with artists since his 2011 Spiral Gallery; he designed a studio for Yue Minjun (who is best known for his intense paintings of himself frozen in laughter), and invited Ding Yi (renowned for his geometric abstraction) to design colorful tiles for the 2014 Artron Arts Center in Shanghai. Liu worked with Zhan Wang on the Blossom Pavilion in 2015 and on the installation of escalators for the Renovation and Reuse of the 80,000-ton Silos in 2017. Liu's collaboration with artists is unique and significant among his peers. The Blossom Pavilion was the first time he had cooperated with Zhan, as part of the Shanghai Urban Space Arts Season (SUSAS) when the latter was experimenting with techniques for the "ground rubbing" (*tadi*, 2015–) project. The project uses the process of the much-valued traditional practice of rubbing stone tablets of highly respected carvings of calligraphy, but radically inverts it to "rub" land in the context of the rapid rise of real estate prices in Beijing. This work was made of thin sheets of stainless steel (0.5 millimeters), measuring precisely one square meter in size, that are beaten with mallets to capture imprints of a piece of ground in the Tongzhou area of Beijing. It carries a price tag of ¥41,314.39, which was the average cost of a square meter of land in that area between 2005 and 2008. Liu Yichun was fascinated by this process and wondered if the six structural supports of the Blossom Pavilion could be wrapped in "slices" of "rubbings" of Chinese rockery so that they would be both there and not there at the same time. In the meantime, a "ghost" of the reflection of the Chinese rockery adds to the tension of the space. Zhan Wang's provocation of the neoliberalist city

↑   *tadi*, 2015– by Zhan Wang
↓   Experimenting with the techniques of "ground rubbing" beneath the escalator

The Return of the Literati

and Liu Yichun's exploration of the limits of building structures do not easily exist side by side as agendas; yet they came together as an experiment. The installation of the bottom panel for the escalators at the 80,000-ton silos also came from Zhan Wang's ground rubbing project. In Shanghai, Zhan Wang's ground rubbing is far more poignant in the vast Huangpu River waterfront renovation project, for which art, public space, real estate development, and commerce are deeply intertwined. Contemporary Chinese artists have produced highly insightful works of art that are valued by museums around the world; this kind of artist–architect collaboration, if history is any guide, will soon expand to the field of architecture. Atelier Deshaus has explored this productive field ahead of many others.

Atelier Deshaus's insistence on using contemporary materials and forms are highly significant; this is distinctive among his literati-minded generation. Yet, every step of the way towards the conceptualization and realization of a project, Atelier Deshaus is guided by deep principles found in Chinese culture. We should perhaps not be surprised; outstanding architects around the world have worked in very similar ways. For Atelier Deshaus to claim that contemporary materials and structures—as well as contemporary history and theory—are Chinese is an immensely important step not yet taken by most Chinese architects, who tend to come down in favor of one side or the other.

MOUNTAIN AND WATER IN THE CITY

Perhaps the greatest challenge for the Chinese city is to develop and maintain public spaces that parallel the example of the Greek *polis* in overcoming an endless variety of family-derived and exclusive spatial encirclement. Public space is the fundamental idea that made the *polis* the most successful concept for the city; we continue to defend and expand this tradition through institutions of truth and justice, knowledge, education, healthcare, finance, and entertainment. Yet the idea of public space is far from intuitive, in fact it is a highly cultivated and vulnerable sensibility. Traditional Chinese cities were constructed around the spaces belonging to the family and institutions—none of which qualify as public space—that were modeled on the archetype of the family. They were most visibly compartmentalized by the use of walls. Today, many areas of Chinese cities are still made of encircled and protected spaces such as the "work unit" *(danwei)* and "gated residential areas" *(xiaoqu)*. The creation of public space has been high on the agenda of reform-minded architects and urbanists in China for over a century; despite the accomplishments of public park systems, urban squares, and shopping districts, certain aspects of public space such as care and politeness are still elusive goals. It is clearly still an evolving brief for China's urban design.

In addition to shopping districts, "artists' villages" have become a particularly successful example of Chinese public space in the twenty-first century for several important reasons: they are somewhat removed from mainstream consumerism, capable of harboring forms of criticality and reflexivity, and maintaining a spatial interest sustained by the adaptive reuse of either existing villages or disused industrial areas. Urbanus, one of the most outstanding practices established in 1999 by its three partners Meng Yan, Liu Xiaodu, and Wang Hui, took on the agenda of developing architecture from the interests of the public city. Their first great success was the renovation of an abandoned factory in Shenzhen known as Overseas Chinese Town (OCT), where they run their office and took the initiative to masterplan an area now filled with unique restaurants, galleries, artist's studios, and fascinating small shops. It is unique, vibrant, stimulating, and public, embodying qualities that inspire a sense of vitality in city life. Urbanus curated the 2017 Bi-City Biennale of Urbanism/Architecture in Shenzhen to focus on the plight of China's urban villages—a rather unique reality resulting from China's rapid urbanization and the different land ownership laws in cities and villages—as "places of resistance" to the relentless occupation of encircled developments. Urbanus was following a trend that began with a successful artists' village in Beijing known as 798, located on the site of a former military factory), which set off the development of many other artists' villages in China, including the short-lived M50 in Shanghai.

For Atelier Deshaus, it is the West Bund that has gripped the urban imagination. Vast parts of the waterfront along Shanghai's Huangpu River, upstream from the Pudong and the Bund, were once industrial and storage areas. Shanghai's 2010 World Expo made the first move to regenerate these riverbanks to the north and south of the city center. When Sun Jiwei, a PhD graduate from Tongji University's School of Architecture, was appointed as the leader of Shanghai's Xuhui District in 2011, he had great ambitions for Shanghai's waterfront and viewed London's South Bank and Herzog de Meuron's Tate Modern as his paradigms. The 2014 Long Museum was the first project begun under his leadership, having persuaded a collector couple, Liu Yiqian and Wang Wei, to invest in an art museum. This was followed by a renovation of an aircraft factory into West Bund Art Center designed by Atelier Deshaus (2014), an aircraft hangar into the Yuz Museum Shanghai designed by Sou Fujimoto, aviation fuel tanks into Tank Shanghai designed by OPEN Architecture (2019), and a railway station into the Start Museum designed by Atelier Jean Nouvel. This was in addition to a range of smaller galleries and design offices such as Atelier Deshaus itself, the intellectual Tong Ming Studio, and a gallery space by Philip Yuan, the great innovator of robotic fabrication with cultural roots. In addition, the first West Bund biennale of art and architecture in 2013 (the predecessor of Shanghai's Urban Space Arts Season or SUSAS for short) contributed Yung Ho Chang's Vertical Glass House and Sharon Johnston and Mark Lee's Pavilion of Six Views (now Shanghai Center of Photography). Within five years, the West Bund has become so successful as a center for the arts that SUSAS gained a tremendous reputation in the art world and has been able to expand to other parts of the Huangpu waterfront, leading to Atelier Deshaus's Renovation and Reuse of 80,000-ton Silos, the Modern Art Museum, and the Riverside Passage, all designed by Atelier Deshaus.

Liu Yichun played a pivotal role in shaping the West Bund, as his Long Museum was a test case that proved the concept. He actively invited small, innovative design firms to move to the West Bund and called the cluster of design firms an "extitute"—an alternative reality to the "institute" *(sheji yuan)* that represented the mainstream of China's architectural design profession—to capture its cultural significance. It is this larger context of Shanghai's urban transformation that brings an enormously important dimension to Liu Yichun's rethinking on the role of the Chinese literati. Unlike Wang Shu and Dong Yugan, who shunned urban commissions, Liu Yichun embraces the city. He rather enjoyed the challenge. The city, of course, is infinitely more complex than a building, and we do not really have a contemporary precedent for a city of the literati. Perhaps this is why Liu Yichun is so motivated to develop a new Chinese, yet public, city. There is a path to the scenario of the "city of the literati"; it is through cultivation, the modification *(xiu)* and nourishment *(yang)* of the body. Here, the care for the body *(xiuyang)* and the care of architecture *(yin, jie, ti, yi)* are not separately conceived; it is exciting to explore this potential when these ideas are transferred to urban design.

One of the most intriguing ideas that the new literati bring to the discussion of urbanism is that of "mountain and water" *(shanshui)*, a generality that stands for the physical environment, and a key concept in poetic painting and writing. Although it has been routinely used in the context of painting, its potential as an urban theory remains underexplored. The historic city of Hangzhou can be understood as a physical manifestation of the concept of *shanshui*, a point that Wang Shu and Wang Xin repeatedly stress. Might Shanghai, with a nudge from Atelier Deshaus, be a place where *shanshui* can be created in the twenty-first-century Chinese city? Among all the instrumental powers possessed by the contemporary city, Atelier Deshaus emphasizes the "acuteness of observation, precision of knowing, and skills of weaving" that could take us to the idea of the urban *shanshui* with a compelling example. Liu Yichun's profound thinking and energizing practices have given us far more to reflect on than the professionalization of architectural practice; Atelier Deshaus has unassumingly begun to speculate and experiment on a path to a different city that could sustain both humility and freedom in the Daoist tradition—but in an age of hubris and environmental destruction.

THE LONG ARCH OF LITERATI TRANSFORMATION

The generation of literati-minded Chinese architects represented by Liu Yichun is concerned neither with revolutionary activism nor with the canonical antiquarianism of early twentieth-century China. They are interested in reinventing a way of life, through architecture, that is in tune with ecological orders. However, two important understandings have to be registered at this point. First, as Jullien reminds us in *Silent Transformations* (2011), change over time is less about ruptures (which underpin history in the European tradition) than about forms of continuity. The "rebirth" of the European Renaissance was a continuity of a spiritual life hybridized with a distant, foreign philosophical tradition from ancient Greece, even though this is much less gripping as a narrative than a rebirth would be. Similarly, the current transformation associated with the return of the literati in China is a process rather than a rupture. Second, in the course of this transformation, the new literati are formulating a modified balance between individual agency, the familial and social collective, and the ecological orders of the planet. This is a complex undertaking, and the agenda of individual agency is prominent even though the resulting practices are different from familiar European and American forms. It is important to bear this in mind before we move too swiftly to Orientalize this development in China.

Despite the complexity of their intellectual position, the new Chinese literati so aptly represented by the works of Atelier Deshaus and Liu Yichun are part of a fundamental reassessment of human life in relation to each other and to the planet. Our current paradigm is the European and American model of rights-holding individuals conducting acts of self-determination and fulfillment. The eminent sociologist Fei Xiaotong spoke of the "other-encompassed self" in the Chinese tradition to define a divergent relationship in Daoism that forms the intellectual context of the literati in their delightful practices relating to art, architecture, and literature. Hu Shi (1891–1862), one of the leading reformers of the Chinese intellectual tradition in the early twentieth century, famously anticipated a "Chinese Renaissance" for his generation; this, however, proved to be elusive and Hu Shi had no notable architectural achievements to lend credence to his claim. A century later, Atelier Deshaus represents a development in China that is much closer in spirit to Hu Shi's pronouncement. If we put aside the narrative of ruptures, this transformation of Chinese culture has already started in architecture—perhaps paralleling the trajectory of the European Renaissance—and may eventually be followed by a similar philosophical transformation.

SELECTED WORKS

01   2003-2005
XIAYU KINDERGARTEN
Huale Road, Qingpu New Town, Shanghai
Floor area: 6,328 m²

Xiayu Kindergarten is situated on the edge of Qingpu New Town. Qingpu is one of the few satellite towns in Shanghai municipality to have retained some of the vernacular residences that are so typical of the Jiangnan watertown region. Qingpu New Town, however, was built as a greenfield development on farmland at some distance from the historic town. Thus, the site of Xiayu Kindergarten palpably lacks the regional architectural influence of a preexisting urban context. Since the site is surrounded by vacant land and absent of any urban ambience, the elevated highway to the east and the river to the west of the site have been a decisive influence on the design instead. Though a source of gas emissions and noise, the elevated highway also allows the new building to be seen at different heights and from different speeds. The river, on the other hand, is a landscape resource that requires both the children's security and the gesture of a piece of riverside architecture to be considered.

The kindergarten has a total of fifteen class units, each of which needs its own activity space, dining area, bedroom, and outdoor playground. These fifteen units and the teachers' offices are clustered together within a massing formed by two curves, with solid and transparent interfaces demarcating the two different uses. The class units are wrapped by curved painted solid walls that extend down to the ground, while the offices and special function rooms are enclosed by U-shaped glass walls elevated above the ground.

Each class unit is designed with the activity room on the first floor to enable direct access to the outdoor playground. The bedroom is located on the second floor, wrapped in a bright colored facade. The bedrooms appear as independent units that are structurally separated from the facade and the roof terrace of the massing below, thereby emphasizing the floating, ambiguous nature of

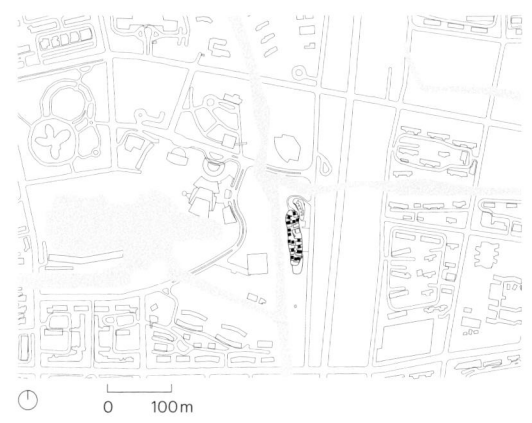

Site plan
West elevation along the riverfront

Atelier Deshaus   Xiayu Kindergarten   36

their individual massing. This ambiguity and detachment of spaces at various scales give the clusters a somewhat "impromptu" feeling. The bedrooms of a group of three class units are connected by elevated passages lined in wood, relating the exterior spaces on the roof terrace to the units. Tall trees are planted in each of the ten courtyards, their crowns entering into a dialog with the colorful box-shaped volumes atop the terrace, and thereby enlivening the architectural image that they are part of.

The first and second floors of the building are interspersed with spaces of different densities. The inward-looking courtyards on the first floor and the outward-looking volumes above combine to form an equilibrium between being open and closed.

01

2003–2005

Atelier Deshaus　　　　　Xiayu Kindergarten　　　　　38

↖   Model   ⤓   Roof terrace
                     ↓   Section 1–1

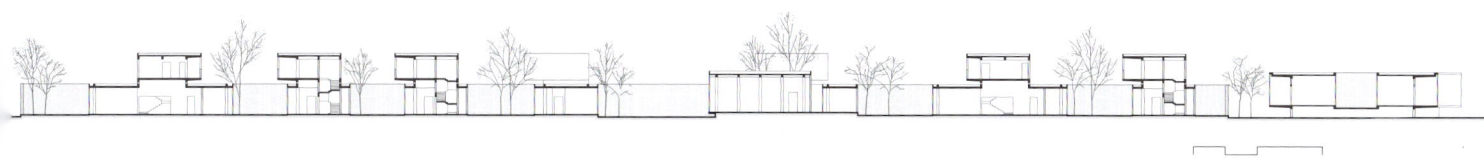

0 5 10   20m

Qingpu New Town, Shanghai, China

01

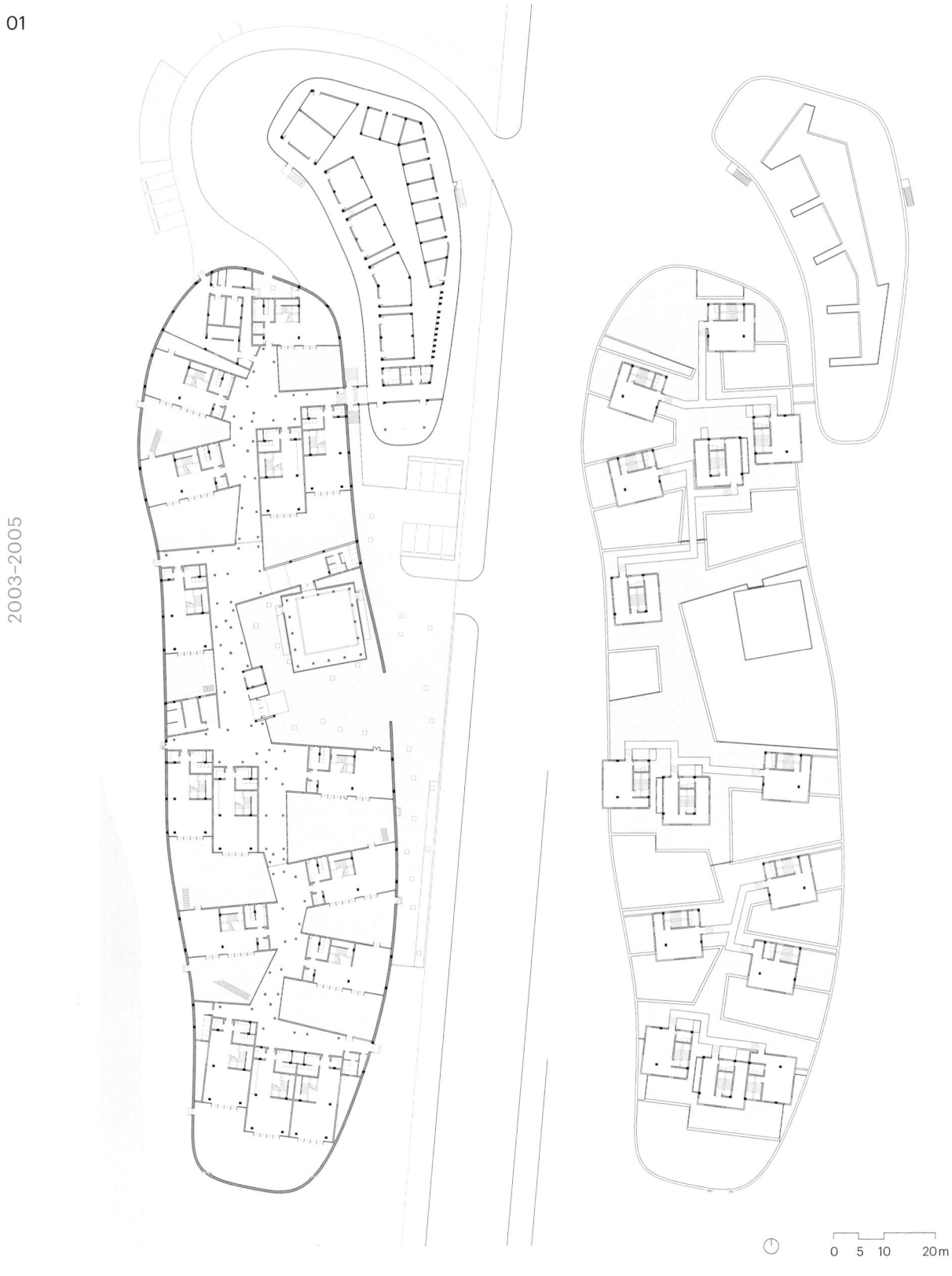

2003-2005

Atelier Deshaus   Xiayu Kindergarten   40

← First-floor plan
← Second-floor plan
↗ West elevation
↘ Northwest elevation

Qingpu New Town, Shanghai, China

01

↑ East elevation
→ Courtyard

Atelier Deshaus					Xiayu Kindergarten					42

Qingpu New Town, Shanghai, China

02 2006-2008
R&D CENTER IN JISHAN SOFTWARE PARK

Jishan, Nanjing, Jiangsu Province
Floor area: 12,000 m²

The R&D Center in Jishan Software Park is located in the beautiful undulating hills of Nanjing's Jiangning district. It provides offices for IT companies in the suburbs, at some distance from the city. Periphery walls enclose an inward-facing courtyard, setting the architecture within its topography. Within the walls, several courtyards and office spaces are linked on the first floor. In contrast, the massing of the offices on the second and third floors are disassembled, each leaning against the periphery walls to reduce the impact on the courtyard below. Inside the courtyards, sequences of thin columns mediate different scales and create the transition between the interior and exterior.

Each courtyard building on the site is integrated into the topography, forming an organic ensemble. The courtyard walls demarcate the interior space while also defining the envelope to the external environment. Whitewash has been used for the courtyard walls. In contrast, the upper floors are wrapped by wooden brise-soleils. The inwardness of the first-floor courtyard and the outwardness of the upper floors together form the architectural "prototype" in this project.

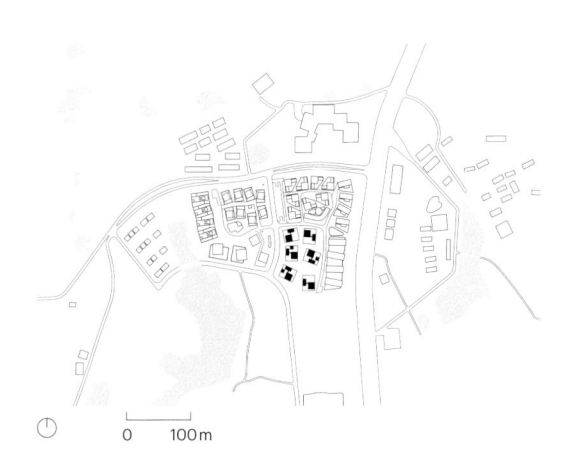

↖ Site plan
↦ View from outside

Jishan, Nanjing, Jiangsu Province, China

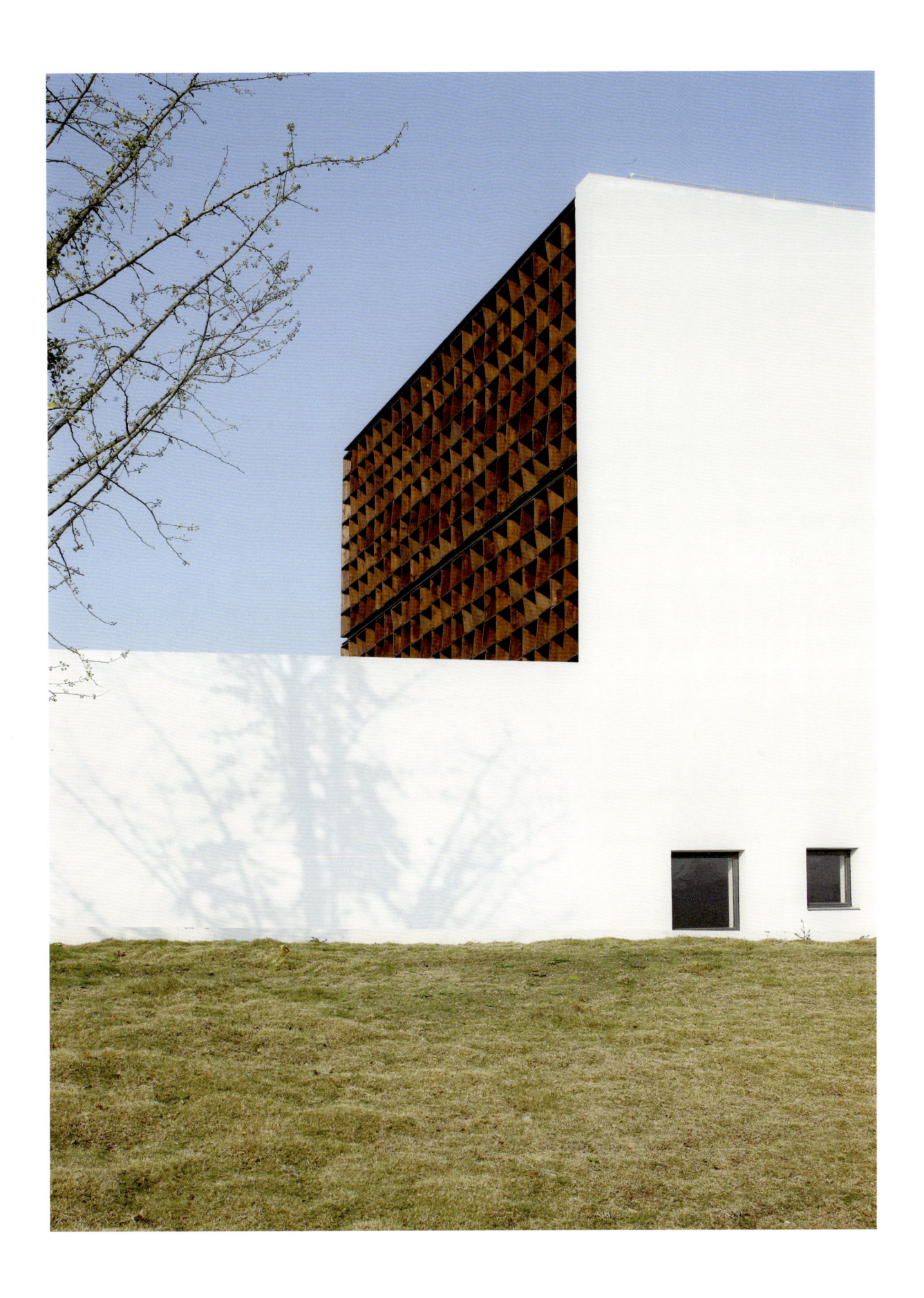

02

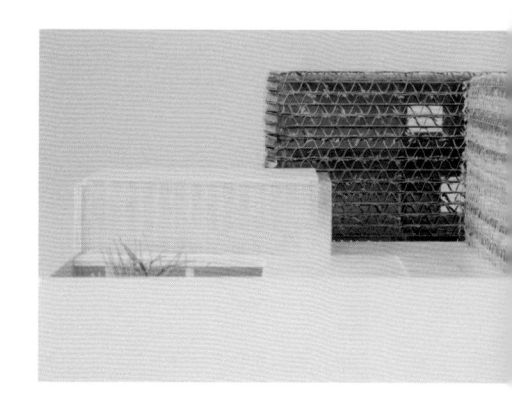

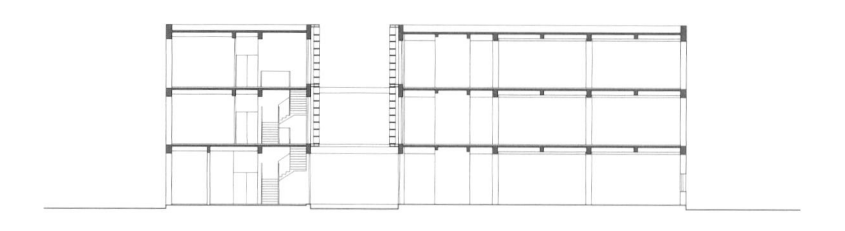

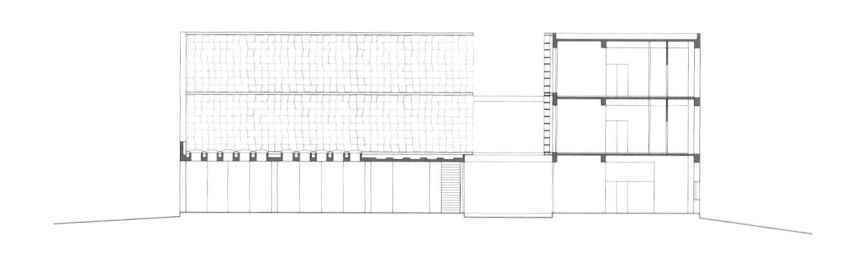

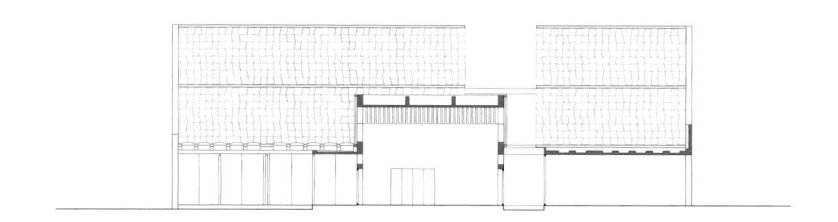

↑ Model
↥ Section 1-1
↧ Section 2-2
↓ Section 3-3

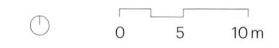

0 5 10 m

Atelier Deshaus   R&D Center in Jishan Software Park   46

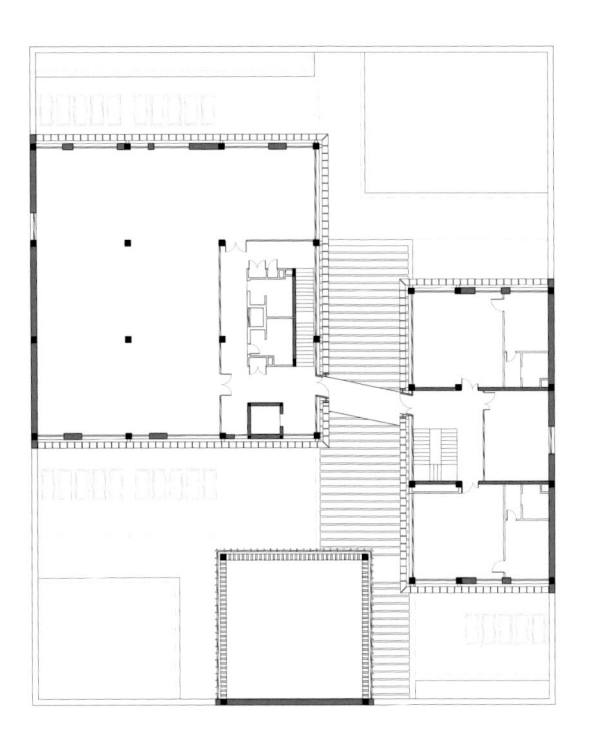

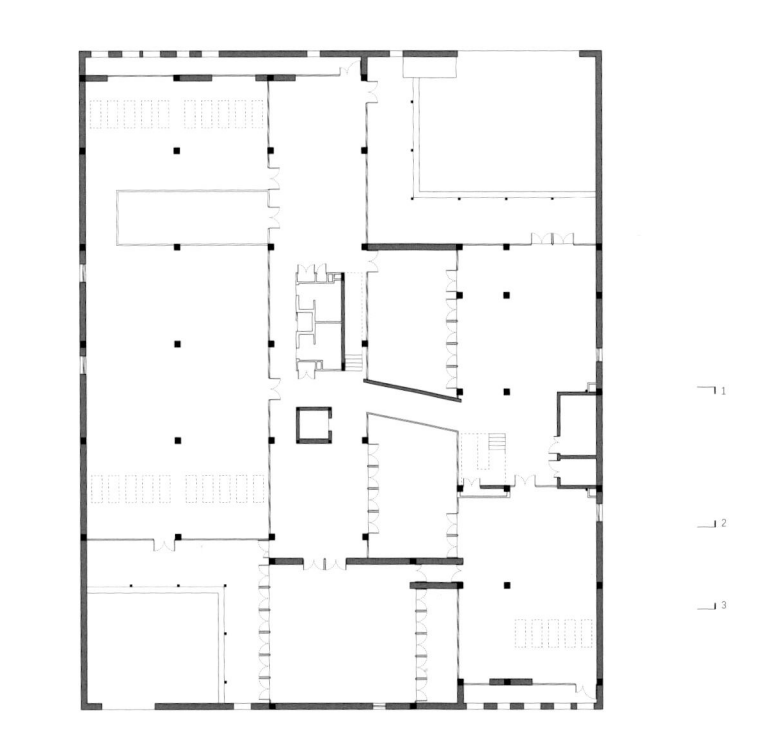

↑ Second-floor plan
↓ First-floor plan

0 5 10 m

Jishan, Nanjing, Jiangsu Province, China

↑ West elevation

Atelier Deshaus   R&D Center in Jishan Software Park

Jishan, Nanjing, Jiangsu Province, China

02

2006–2008

↑ View from southeast
↙ Inner courtyard

↗ Wooden brise-soleils
↘ Buildings along the undulating hills

Atelier Deshaus   R&D Center in Jishan Software Park   50

Jishan, Nanjing, Jiangsu Province, China

03   2008-2010
KINDERGARTEN IN JIADING NEW TOWN

Hongde Road, Jiading, Shanghai
Gross floor area: 6,600 m²

The New Town Kindergarten In Jiading New Town is sited on an open field in the northern suburbs of Shanghai. This proposal differs from our usual design strategy of breaking down and dispersing massing. Rather a strong monolithic form is proposed to carry its own weight on the vast site. This singular form is chosen, because in the orderly road grid of the urban master plan, the proposal's future relationship with adjacent buildings could be anticipated.

The architecture is formed by two elongated north–south volumes. The northern volume is the main circulation space, with a hall linking the ramps to the different levels. The southern volume is for the kindergarten functions, containing fifteen class units, each with activity space and bedrooms, and shared class spaces.

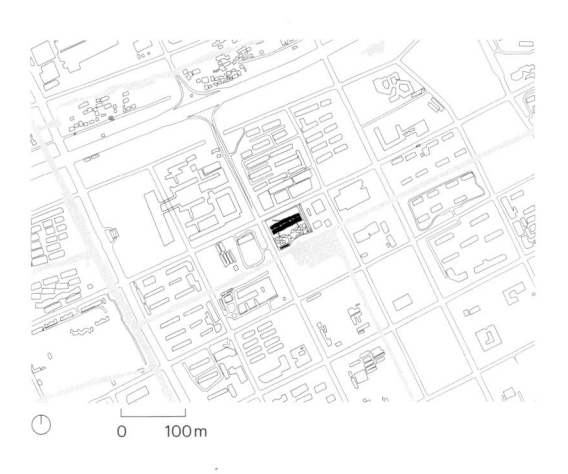

↖   Site plan
↪   The lit-up aluminum facade

The northern atrium with ramps linking the levels offers a space transcending daily life. It is a dynamic and exciting space through which each child passes, upon entering the building every day, to proceed on to his or her classroom. It is a deliberately scaled-up stairwell, and recalls the experience of scholar rock in traditional Chinese gardens. The shifting levels in the atrium are reflected on the southern facade of the kindergarten. While these shifts as revealed on the facade lend the building a dynamism, outdoor activity spaces are also placed within the concave plan-level shifts that coincide where the level changes occur in section. On the one hand, shifting levels are thus visible on the facade; on the other hand, there is a shift from the tradition of expansion in the horizontal direction in a courtyard spatial organization to an expansion also in the vertical direction, rendering the activities of the children and the atrium part of the facade.

Jiading, Shanghai, China

03

2008-2010

↑ South elevation
↓ North elevation

Atelier Deshaus   Kindergarten in Jiading New Town   54

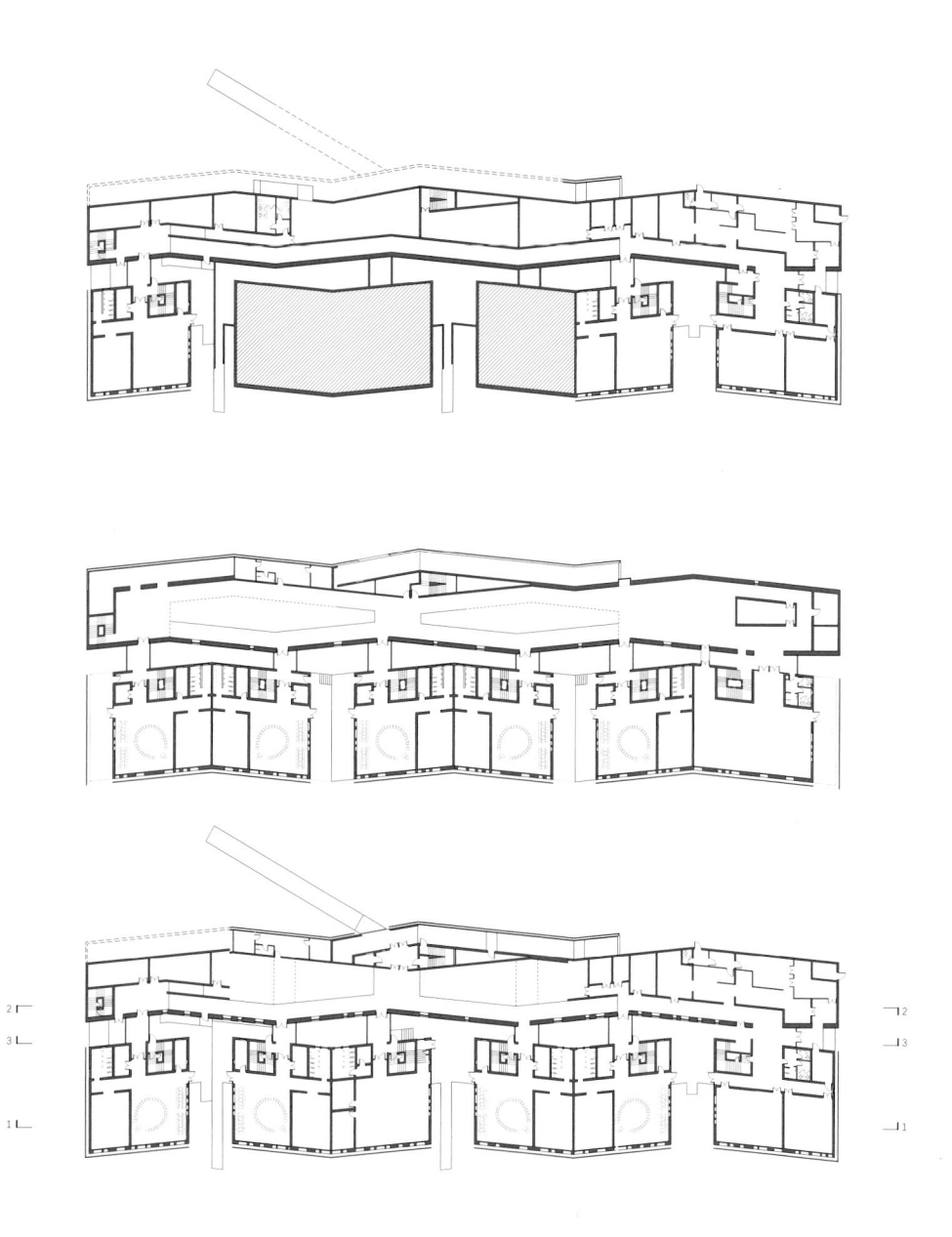

↑ Third-floor plan
∅ Second-floor plan
↓ First-floor plan

0 5 10 20m

Jiading, Shanghai, China

55

03

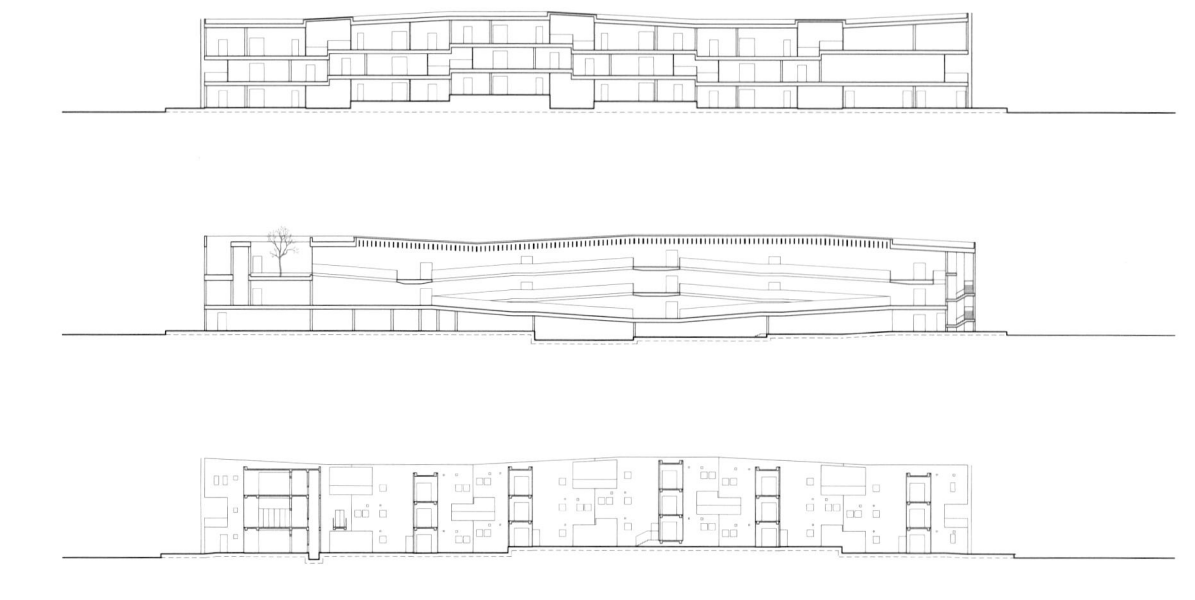

2008–2010

↑ Section 1–1
∅ Section 2–2
↓ Section 3–3

0 5 10   20m

Atelier Deshaus   Kindergarten in Jiading New Town   56

↑　　　Model

Jiading, Shanghai, China

03

2008–2010

↳ Ramps around the central atrium

Atelier Deshaus   Kindergarten in Jiading New Town   58

↑　　　South elevation detail

Jiading, Shanghai, China

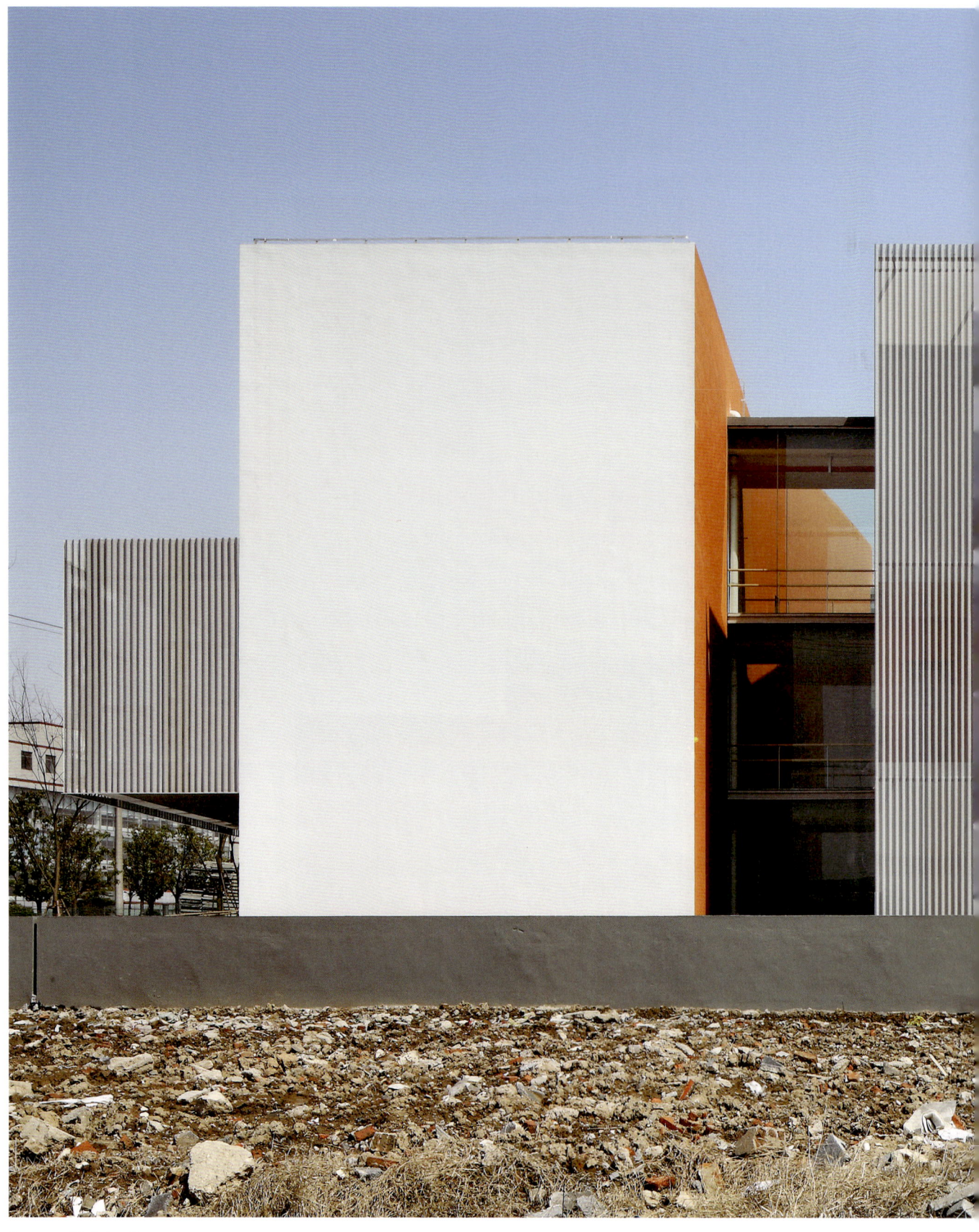

↑ West elevation

Jiading, Shanghai, China

04   2009–2012
QINGPU YOUTH CENTER

Huake Road, Qingpu, Shanghai
Gross floor area: 6,612 m²

The Youth Center is located in a new town in the eastern part of the township of Qingpu. A shift in the modes of mobility and demographic growth mean that Qingpu's new town, in comparison with the old town, is characterized by less of a fine-grained scale, and by wide straight roads and large architectural setbacks. Standardized and technical planning controls make the urbanism of the new town seem monotonous and inhospitable.

On the main roads of the new town, the fine human-scale space of the traditional Jiangnan watertowns has been all but lost. But imprints of the historical Jiangnan can still be found in secondary public spaces such as in the gardens of Beijing Park, the creek south of the School of Administration, the creek along Huaqing Road, and the as-yet undemolished Xiayang village and its fish ponds. These places remind us that the potential for fine-grained human-scale public spaces does exist despite the pressures of large-scale urbanism.

The design for the Youth Center takes its different functions, disintegrates them into small-scale massings according to their uses, and then connects them through courtyards, small plazas, lanes, and other outdoor spaces to form a cluster. The activities of the young people inside the architectural spaces—moving between the different programmatic spaces, wandering carefree and making unexpected discoveries—are like activities in a small city. Reacting to the magnification of the urban scale accompanying the urbanization process in the peripheral spaces, the design uses fine-grained and humanizing public spaces to evoke memories of traditional urbanism. Dynamic, human-scale outdoor spaces also resonate with the sensibility of the young people and their activities. A building can also be a miniature city.

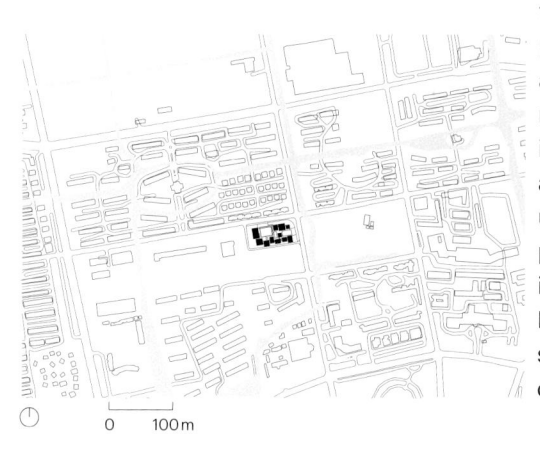

↖ Site plan
↱ North elevation

Qingpu, Shanghai, China

↑   Aerial view

Atelier Deshaus   Qingpu Youth Center   64

Qingpu, Shanghai, China

04

2009–2012

↑ Garden in courtyard
↗ The water yard
→ Alley in the rain

Atelier Deshaus Qingpu Youth Center 66

Qingpu, Shanghai, China

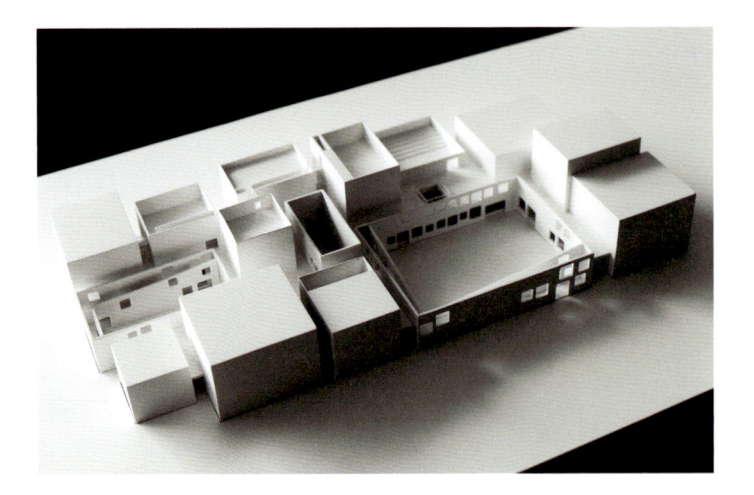

↑ The lit-up facade
↓ Model

↗ Third-floor plan
ø Second-floor plan
↘ First-floor plan

Atelier Deshaus　　　Qingpu Youth Center　　　68

Qingpu, Shanghai, China

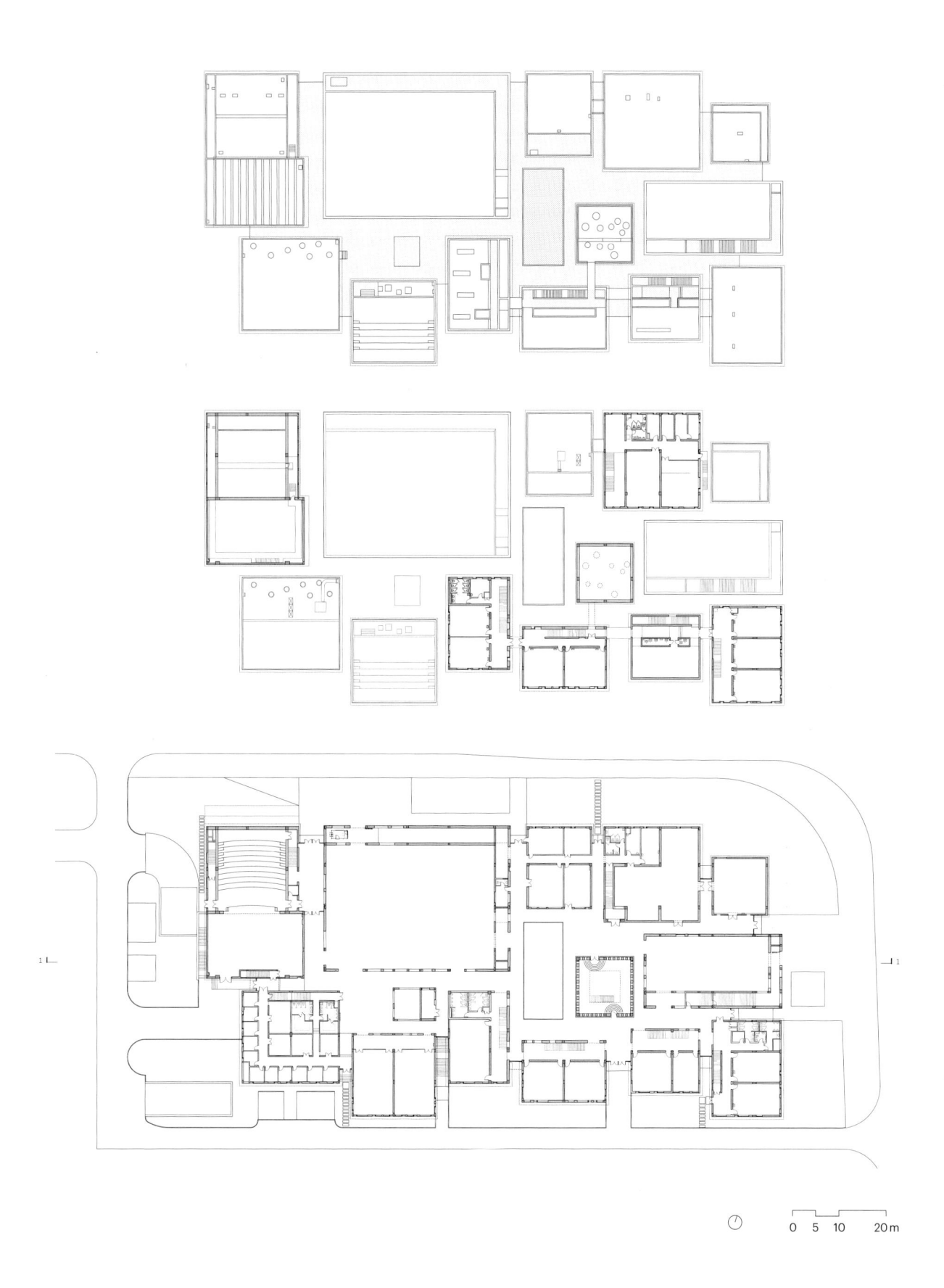

04

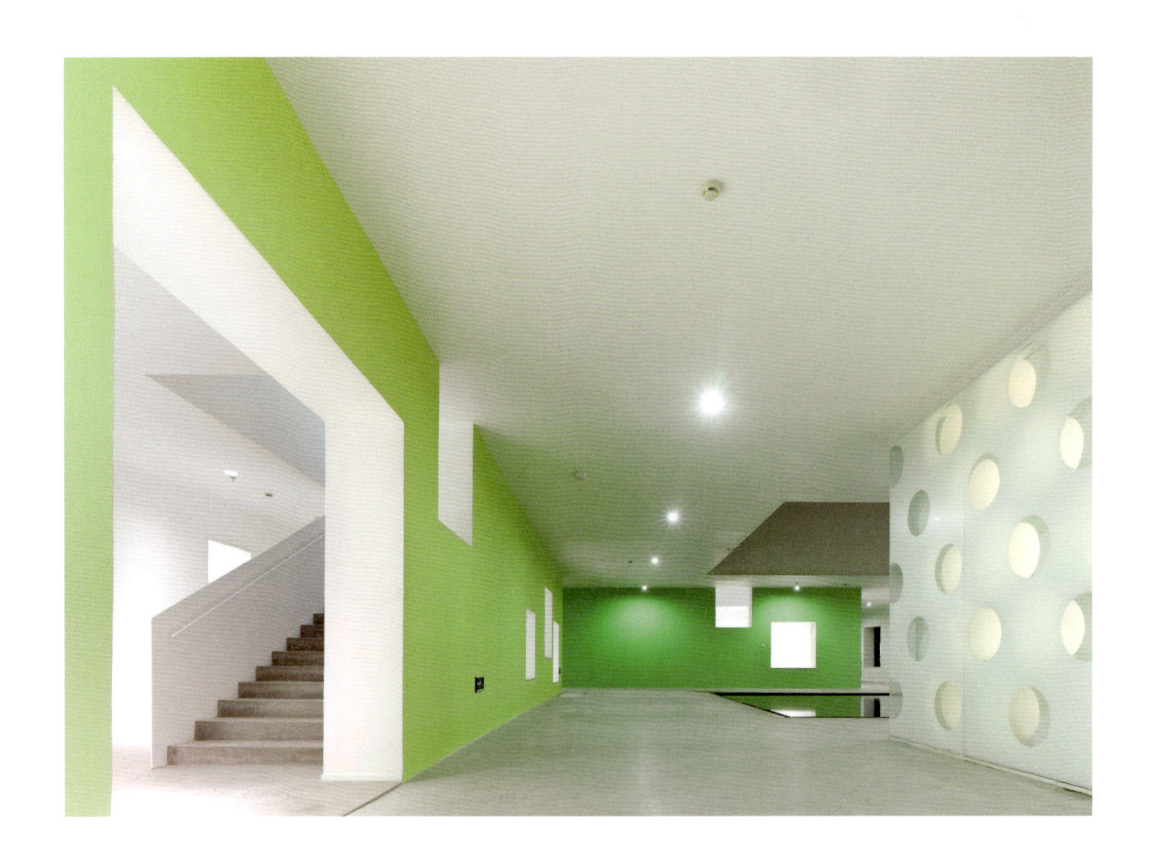

2009–2012

↑ Interior corridor
↓ Roof terrace

Atelier Deshaus   Qingpu Youth Center   70

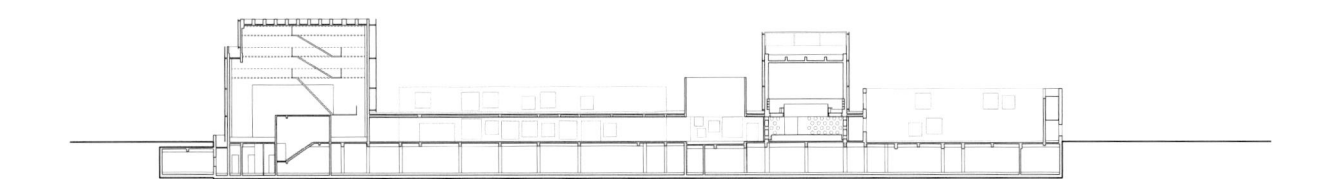

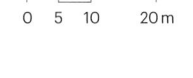

↑   Section 1–1
↓   Library

Qingpu, Shanghai, China

05   2009–2011
SPIRAL GALLERY I

Tianzhu Road, Jiading, Shanghai
Gross floor area: 250 m²

When the Spiral Gallery project was at the design stage there was still wilderness all around the site in the suburbs of Shanghai, with high-rises and roads under construction in the surrounding area. The concept for the gallery, in Jiading New Town's recently developed Central Park, envisaged it as a structure surrounded by woods and large trees. It is very typical for contemporary China that the architecture and its surrounding context were created at the same time.

The design proposal was based on an overall vision of architecture set within its context. A roughly circular shape is punctured by a spiral passage that gradually shifts from compressed to more open to intimate, before finally arriving at the inner courtyard where it is possible to enter the interior space. The interior space carved out by the spiral passage also changes its character from spacious to private as it opens out onto the inner courtyard. In the plan, two lines spiral towards the center. Although they travel parallel to each other, they also form a continuous space with a shifting width, in the process defining specific spatial relationships. Service areas such as the washroom, kitchen, storage, small bedrooms, offices, etc., are located between the spaces enclosed by the spiral. In contrast, the space outside the spiral is freed up and holds the potential for flexible functionality. The two spiral lines also create two intertwined spaces: One is inside the gallery, while the other is the roof surface created by the rising terrain inside the spirals. The spatial sequence continues and ultimately arrives back at its starting point.

↖   Site plan
↱   Courtyard overview

The architectural concept was inspired by the spiral shape, which both sets a spatial framework and creates a new way of entering the building from the surrounding area. A visitor can choose to enter the building directly or to walk up the stairs and then descend into the central courtyard, thereby accessing the interior through the experience of shifting viewpoints, sight lines, and visual heights. As the visitor alternates between open and enclosed views on this deliberately extended stroll, the surrounding landscape also becomes part of the architecture, which is an abstraction of the techniques used in traditional Chinese gardens.

Looking out at the landscape thus becomes a way of entering the architecture—and conversely, architecture exists too for the sake of the landscape.

Jiading, Shanghai, China

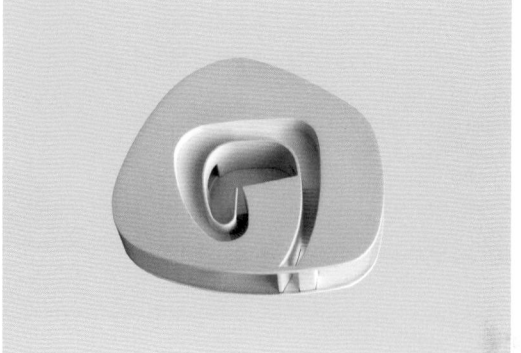

↑ Model
↖ Stairs

Atelier Deshaus Spiral Gallery 74

↑ Courtyard with curved wall   ↑ Evening view

Jiading, Shanghai, China

↑ Roof terrace and the surrounding scenery

Jiading, Shanghai, China

05

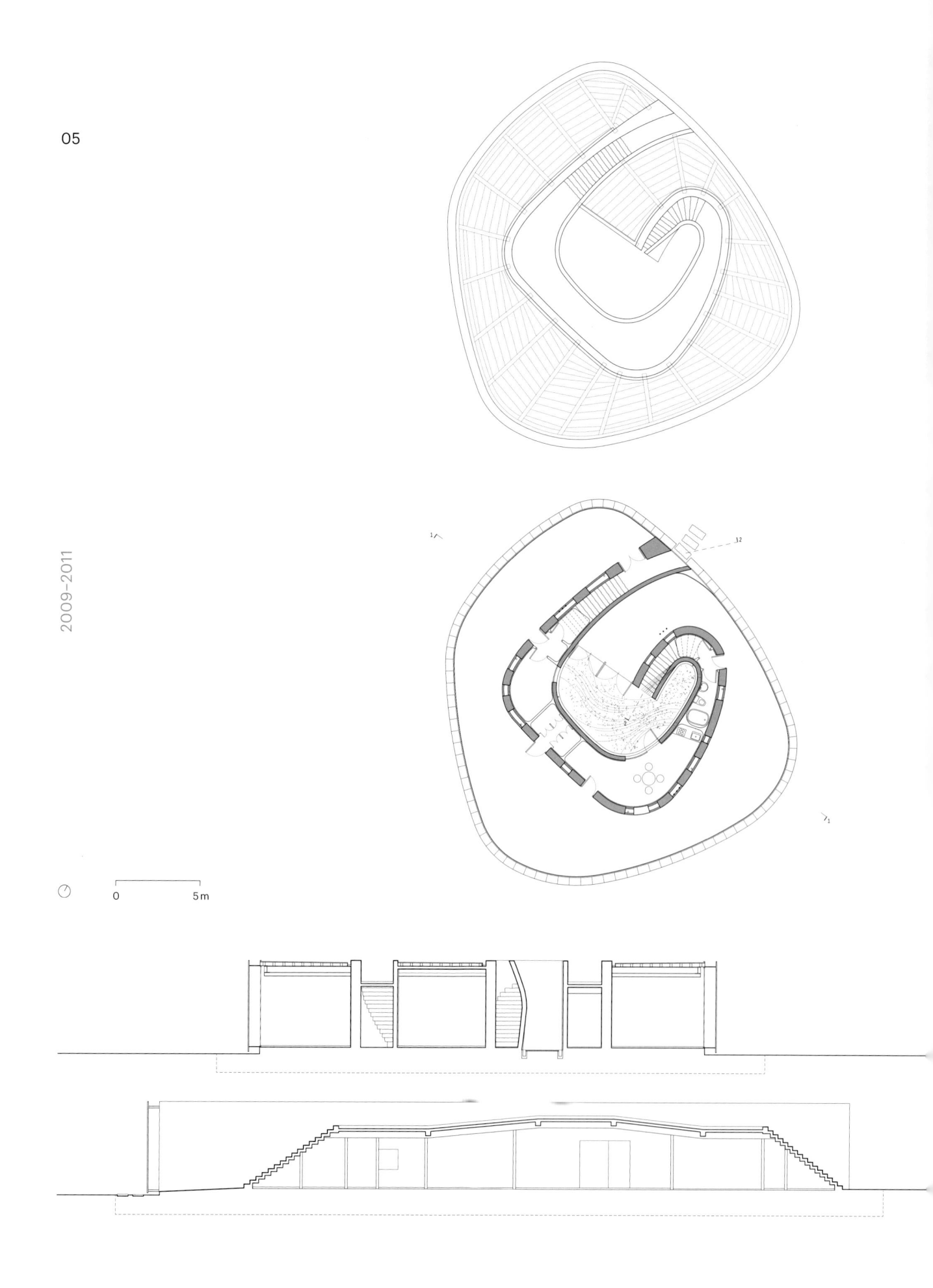

2009–2011

0   5m

Atelier Deshaus   Spiral Gallery   78

↖ Roof plan of wooden purlins
↖ First-floor plan
← Section 1-1
↙ Section 2-2
↑ Courtyard detail
→ Courtyard

Jiading, Shanghai, China

06   2010–2015
SHANGHAI INTERNATIONAL AUTOMOBILE CITY R&D CENTER

Anhong Road, Jiading, Shanghai
Gross floor area: 36,600 m²

Situated in the northwest of Shanghai in the new town of Anting, this was a project that aimed to create a facility for the automobile industry with the focus on research and development (R&D). Covering a total construction area of 150,000 square meters, it was one of five parcels on the site to have been commissioned for design.

A masterplan outlined the overall layout of each parcel as well as the building footprint and the number of floors in each building. However, the design requirements for each building remained quite vague: a rough breakdown was given of the space needed for prototyping and for research and development, but no other detailed requirements were specified. The site resembled many others in the suburban new towns of constantly changing Chinese cities, and the sense of alienation within the generic setting similarly offered little reference for design.

In order to find a sense of belonging in spite of this alienation, the design relied on a basic strategy of redefining each building as a kind of settlement with multiple layers of the environment. Each settlement is made up of two vertically overlapping spaces for R&D and prototyping. The R&D spaces occupy the second to fourth floors, with an elongated internal plaza below that is also the "center" of each settlement, flanked on each side by R&D units. The R&D units are intentionally stepped back incrementally from this internal plaza, which also opens the plaza vertically along both the planar length and depth. Moreover, the step-back of the R&D units creates layered terraces that are linked by exterior staircases to create a lively whole, forming an organic extension of the central plaza. Researchers can use these spaces for relaxing, communicating, and holding events. The first floor is used for prototyping, equipment storage, and services, and is divided into eight volumes of different

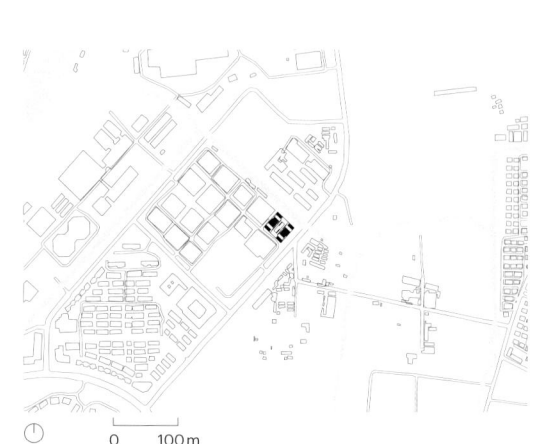

0 100 m

↖   Site plan
↪   Aerial view

sizes. These volumes are organized around inner courtyards and separated from each other by a corridor for logistics and circulation that is at least four meters wide. In contrast to the R&D spaces above, which are well-lit, spatially defined, orderly, and open to the sky, the spaces below are cavernous, more spatially ambiguous, organizationally complex, and seem to hover above the ground.

↑   Inner courtyard and layers of platforms

Anhong Road, Jiading, Shanghai, China

06

Atelier Deshaus — Shanghai International Automobile City R&D Center

← Manufacturing laboratories on the first floor
↗ Inner courtyard and the manufacturing laboratories
↘ Inner courtyard and layers of platforms

Anhong Road, Jiading, Shanghai, China

06

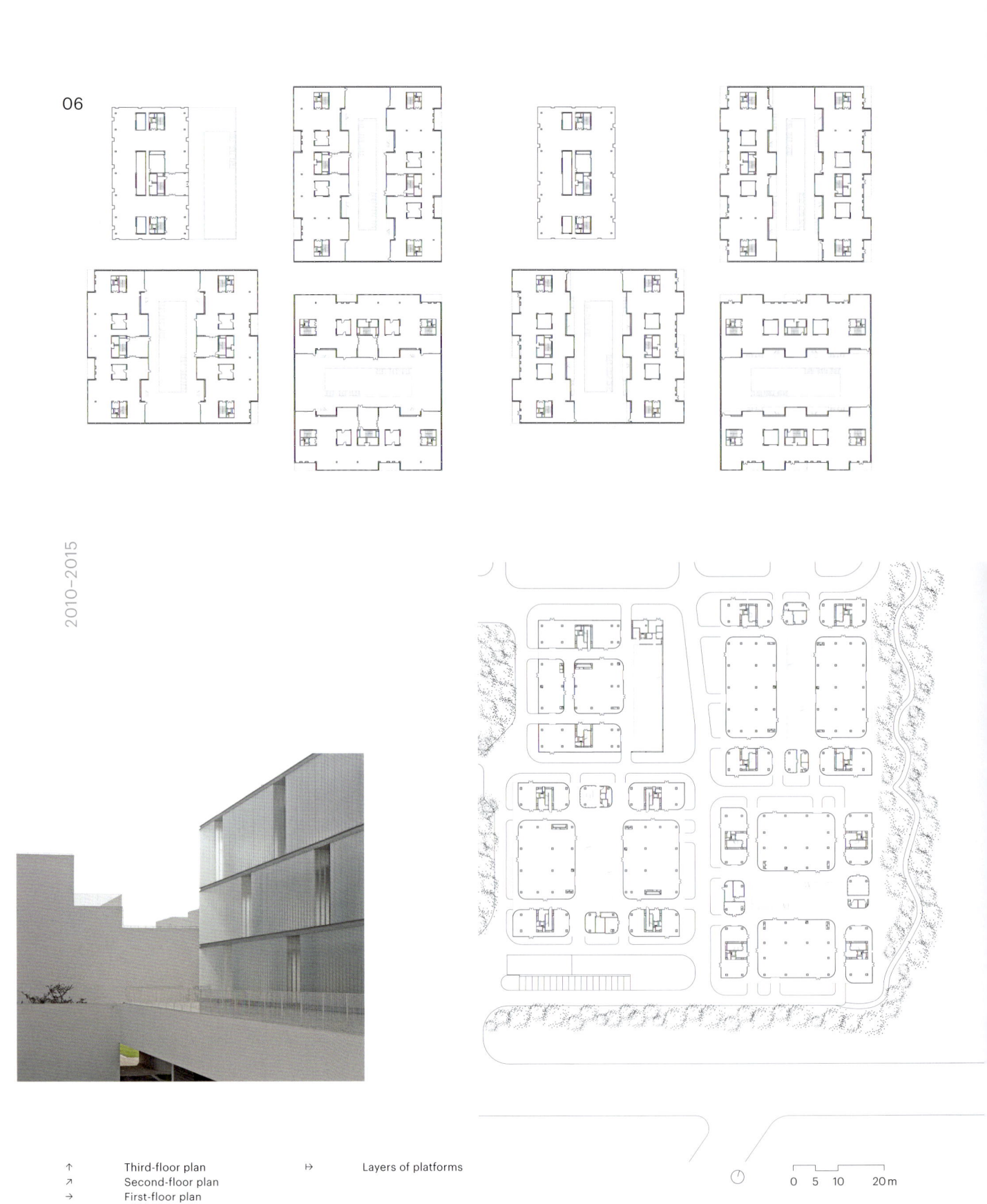

↑ Third-floor plan
↗ Second-floor plan
→ First-floor plan
↵ View from the terrace

↦ Layers of platforms

0 5 10   20 m

Atelier Deshaus   Shanghai International Automobile City R&D Center   86

Anhong Road, Jiading, Shanghai, China

↑ The terrace with R&D cubes

↑ View from outside

Anhong Road, Jiading, Shanghai, China

07 2010–2015
TAO LI YUAN SCHOOL IN JIADING

Shuping Road, Jiading, Shanghai
Floor area: 35,688 m²
Site area: 57,495 m²

Tao Li Yuan School relocated from the densely packed old town to a new setting in the New Development Zone northwest of Jiading. Occupying a site that is surrounded on the north, east, and west by new roads planned for the future new town, and on the south by a creek, only the as-yet undemolished parts of the village and its surrounding farmlands across the creek bear the historic characteristics that are so typical of Jiangnan watertowns.

In response to the vanishing spatial culture of Jiangnan watertowns, the design takes the school's specific functions and uses the architectural element of the courtyard to recall the spatial form of traditional Jiangnan academies, thereby offering the pupils a school campus with regional characteristics that brings together learning and freedom. This educational facility comprises an elementary school (with five grades and 25 classrooms) and a junior high school (with four grades and 32 classrooms). Each courtyard is thus designed for one grade, with its functional and spatial layers overlapping vertically. Special classrooms and the teachers' offices are on the first floor while the ordinary classrooms are on the upper levels. A terraced platform above the first floor serves as a demarcation line, with various educational activities taking place below and conventional teaching happening above this point.

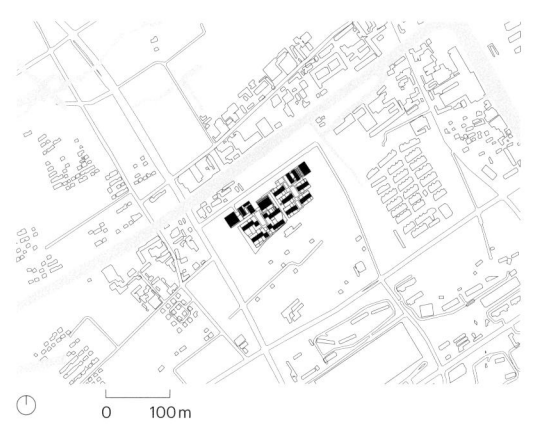

0 100m

↖ Site plan
↱ Aerial view

Atelier Deshaus   Tao Li Yuan School in Jiading   90

The terraced platform is built with a concrete slab structure that extends above the ground floor to form all-weather activity spaces which could flexibly extend outdoors for open-air teaching, while also functioning as connections between the courtyards. This raised platform integrates the entire first-floor level of the campus into an ensemble of courtyards. Quiet study spaces are enclosed within the walls, while leisure activities take place outside, where open courtyards are formed between enclosed ones. The use of verandas also extends the courtyard walls and connects the campus, opening up freely while the rhythmic changes in direction along the veranda recall the classical academies of bygone times.

07

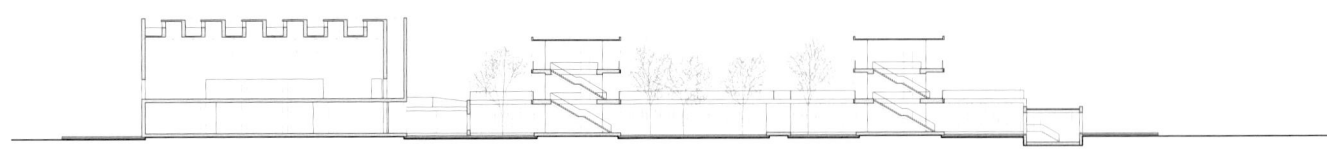

2010–2015

↑ Corridor in the elementary school
↓ Section 1-1

→ Courtyard in junior high school
↳ Elementary school from afar

0 5 10   20 m

Atelier Deshaus   Tao Li Yuan School in Jiading   92

Shuping Road, Jiading, Shanghai, China 93

↑   Elevated platforms of the elementary school
↓   Second-floor plan

Atelier Deshaus   Tao Li Yuan School in Jiading

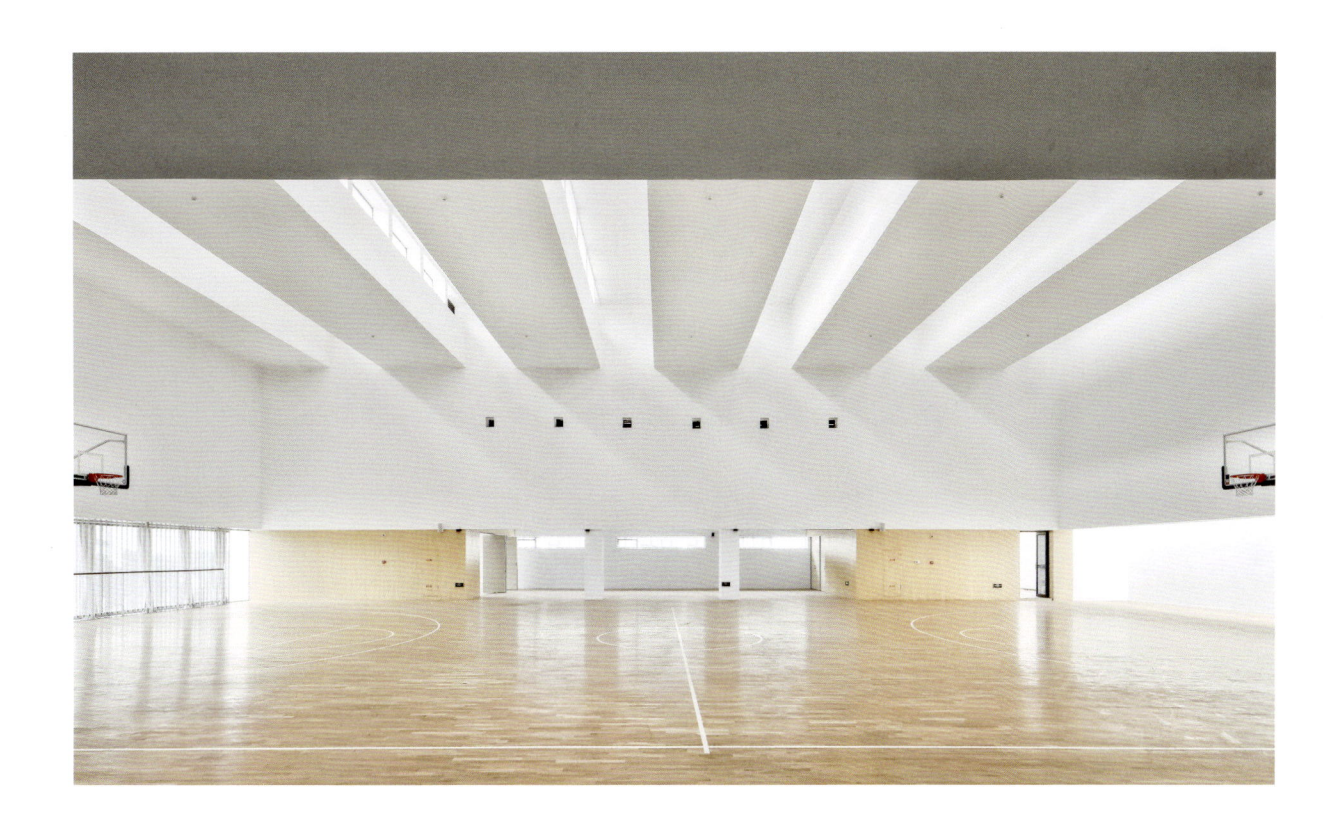

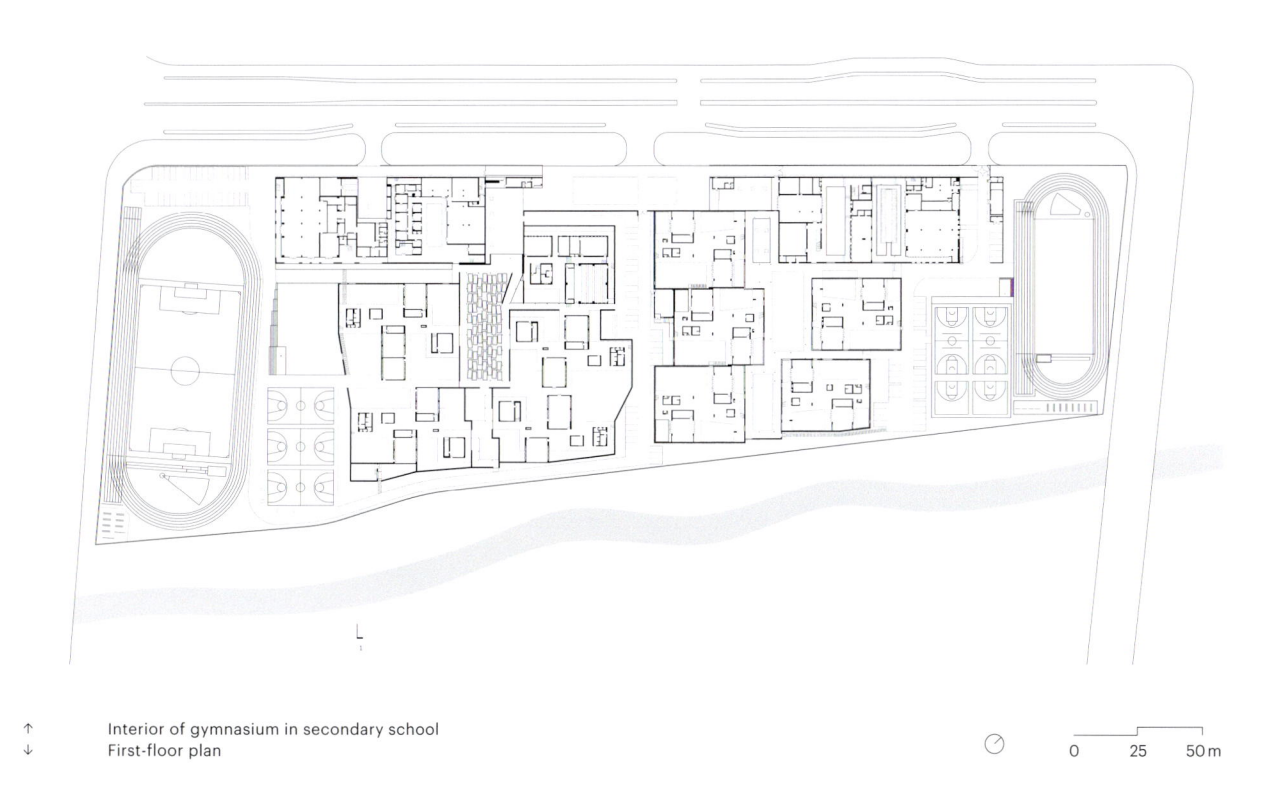

↑ Interior of gymnasium in secondary school
↓ First-floor plan

Shuping Road, Jiading, Shanghai, China

↑ Main courtyard of the junior high school

Atelier Deshaus Tao Li Yuan School in Jiading

Shuping Road, Jiading, Shanghai, China

08   2011–2014

LONG MUSEUM WEST BUND

Longteng Avenue, Xuhui District, Shanghai
Gross floor area: 33,007 m²

Located in Xuhui District in Shanghai, the site for Long Museum West Bund was originally a coal wharf on the Huangpu River. A 1950s loading bridge with coal hoppers has been preserved, measuring about 110 meters long, ten meters wide, and eight meters high. Adjacent to the bridge is a two-story underground parking garage that was built two years before plans for the museum began. This is the sole surviving part of a building whose floors above the ground were never realized.

The new design reuses and develops the potential left by the column grid of 8.4 meters by 8.4 meters, which is the legacy of the standard spatial optimization of the original underground parking garage. Free-floating wall structures inside the space give the exhibition visitors an experience of promenading while fulfilling the new museum's functional brief. These dispersed, autonomous walls are formed by cast-in-situ fair-faced concrete. Each rises vertically and extends out to form umbrella-vaulted canopies. A horizontal sliver visibly separates one unit of a cantilevered umbrella-vault structure from the next.

These walls extending down from the first floor land in the existing column grid of the basement structure. The configuration of the shear walls thus transforms the basement level into an exhibition space, too. The sub-basement remains as parking, with only some of the walls extending to the parking floor as needed. The mechanical system is integrated into the cavity between the walls of the vault-umbrella units, freeing up the interior as an uninterrupted space for exhibitions. The vertical wall and the horizontal ceiling, both of which are made by fair-faced concrete on the surface, are smoothed by the transition of the half oval vault. The horizontal ceiling appears only minimally in the interior.

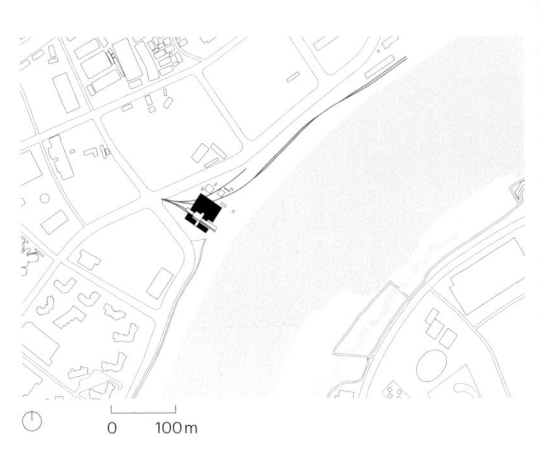

↖   Site plan
↦   The coal hoppers before the transformation

Xuhui District, Shanghai, China

08

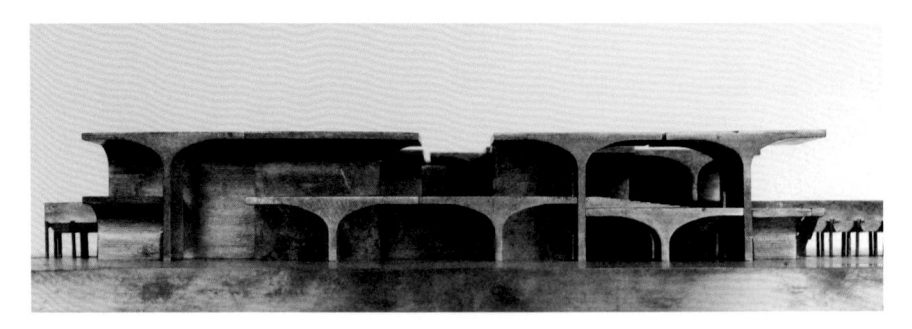

The integration of the structure, the mechanical system, and the spatial image together form the "volumetric structure." In this respect, there is a clarity of intention as well as a direct expression of tectonics and structure in its architectural form, which is analogous to the architectural form of the coal loading bridge on the original industrial site.

↑ The museum in snow
↗ Model
→ Site plan
↪ Northwest elevation
↳ Southwest elevation

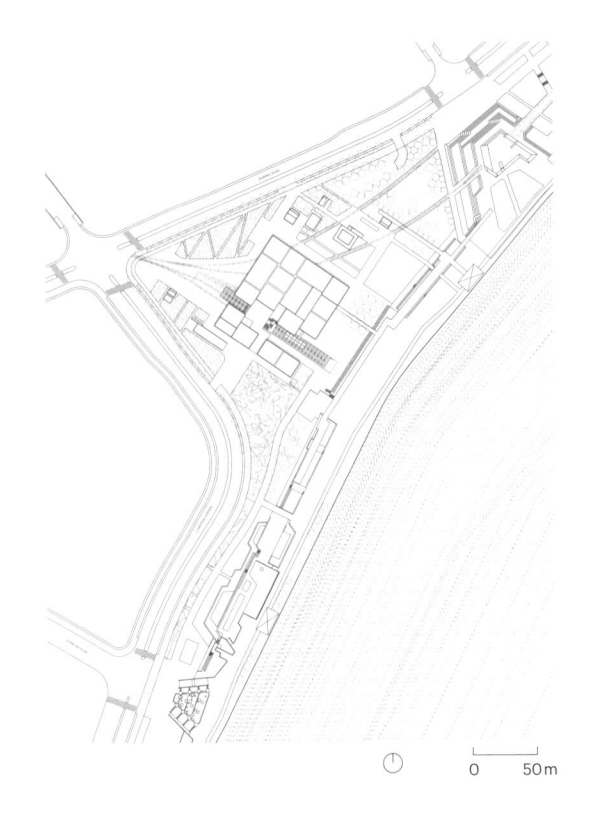

Xuhui District, Shanghai, China

↑ Aerial view

Xuhui District, Shanghai, China

08

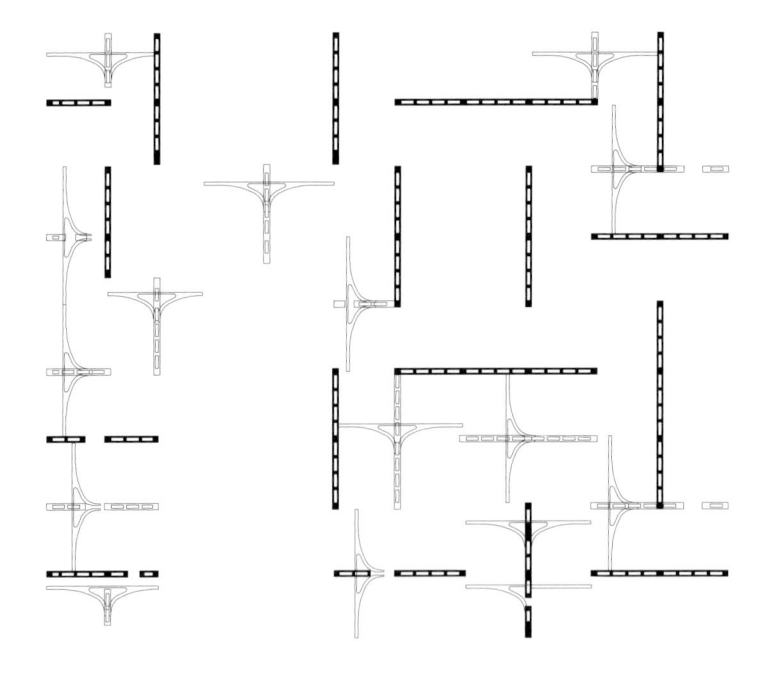

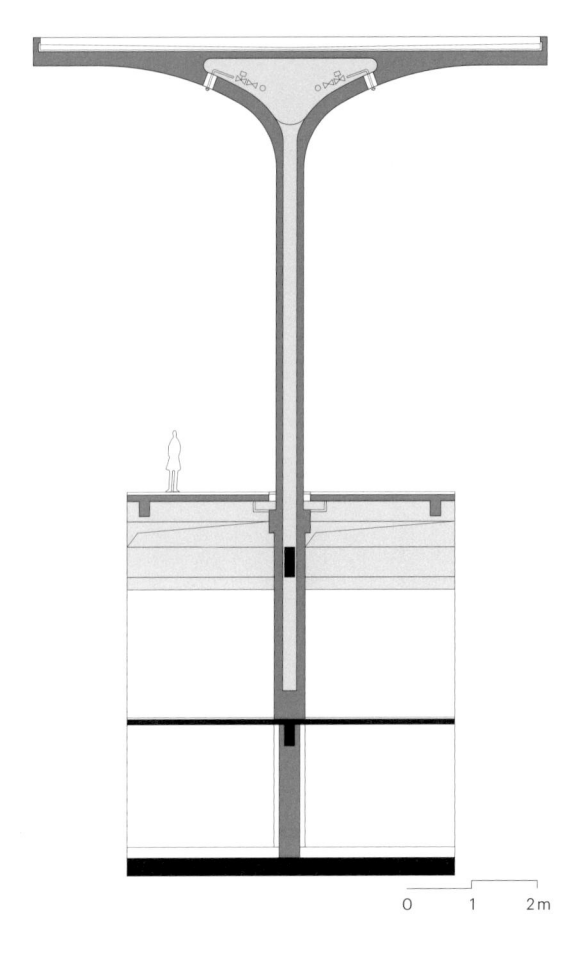

Atelier Deshaus Long Museum West Bund 104

↖ Structural layout
↤ Interior view in the underground art gallery
← Vault umbrella unit
↑ Model

Xuhui District, Shanghai, China

Atelier Deshaus   Long Museum West Bund   106

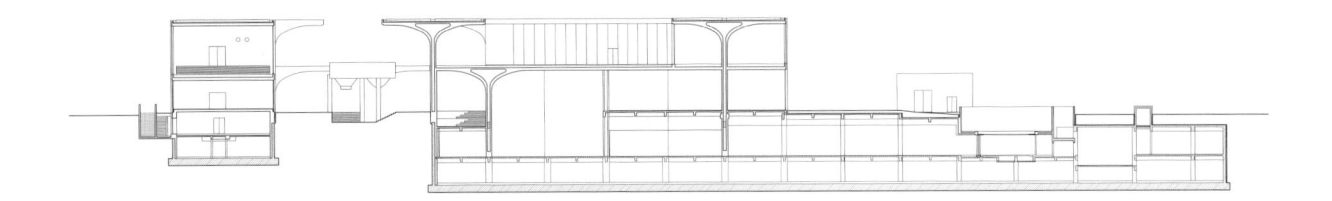

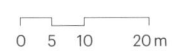

← Semi-underground art gallery
↵ Underground art gallery
↑ Section 1–1
↓ Gallery on the first floor

Xuhui District, Shanghai, China

↑ Entrance

Atelier Deshaus Long Museum West Bund 108

↑   Main exhibition hall

Xuhui District, Shanghai, China

08

2011–2014

↑ First-floor plan
→ Second-floor plan
↪ B1 floor plan
↳ B2 floor plan

0 5 10 20m

Atelier Deshaus   Long Museum West Bund   110

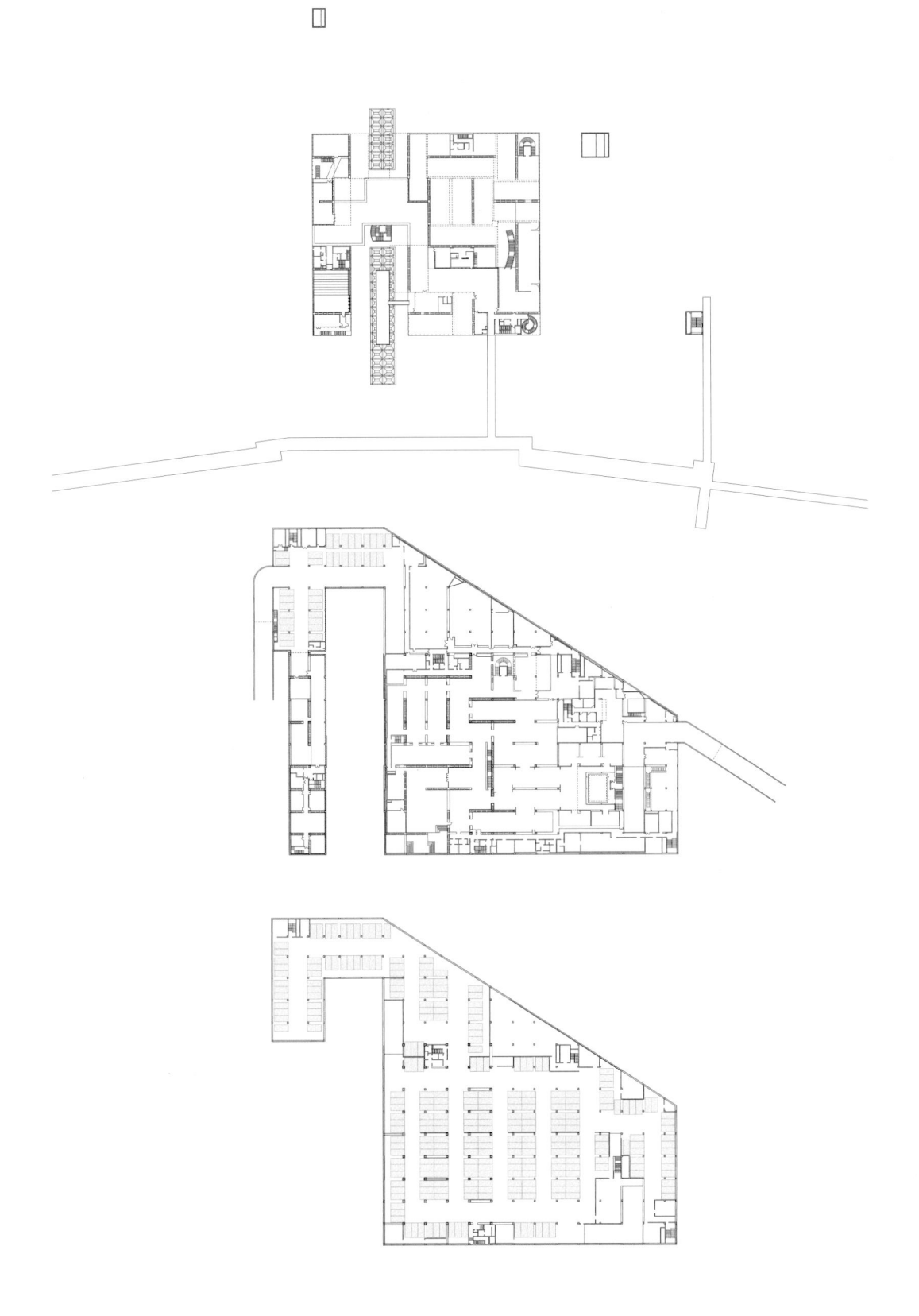

Xuhui District, Shanghai, China

↑ Semi-underground art gallery

Atelier Deshaus Long Museum West Bund

Xuhui District, Shanghai, China

09 2013–2015
HUAXIN CONFERENCE HUB

Tianlin Road, Xuhui District, Shanghai
Gross floor area: 1,000 m²

Located in a dense and tight site within the Huaxin Science and Tech Park, surrounded by pedestrian walkways, parking lots, and office buildings, the design proposal instead takes on the existing congestion as an opportunity for the 1,000-square-meter built area for the Huaxin Conference Hub building.

The design strove for a strategy of overall balance: a hovering concrete wall encloses the inside without entirely disconnecting from the surroundings outside, and four discrete program-specific massings in a windmill-like arrangement are wrapped by this wall.

To mitigate the massing from being oversized, circulation spaces are exteriorized as much as possible. The interstitial spaces between the four volumes are not only connected to the Tech Park, but also the atrium of the Conference Hub. The experience of walking through the Conference Hub alternates between being inside and being outside, and the transitory feeling of being "inside/outside." The walls of the interior spaces are fair-faced concrete, while the walls of the circulation space are painted white. This contrast again highlights the shifts between inside and outside.

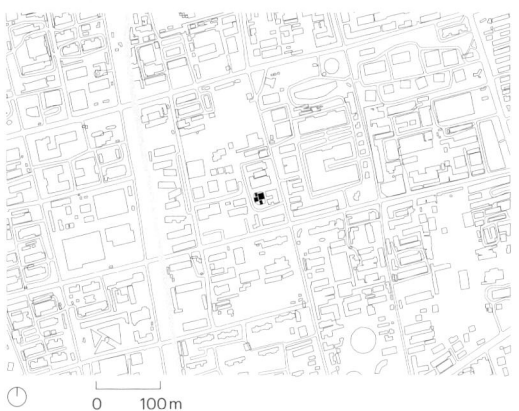

↖ Site plan
↦ The hub connected to the office building by an overbridge

To control the overall height of the building, the ground is sunk by 1.5 meters inside the periphery wall, while the sloped retaining wall still allows for a continuity with the surroundings. Through this gesture, the two floors are at split levels with the ground of the Tech Park. Standing on any of the levels, one is able to perceive the existence of the other two levels – a transitoriness in perceiving the "upper or lower" level is thus formed.

Even though the Conference Hub is massive, the wall enclosure that is hovering off the ground visually lightens its heaviness. The painting of the fair-faced concrete in white, similarly, effects this transience between lightness and heaviness. The shifts, in plan, of the four masses in relation to each other and the outward tilt of the exterior wall further express the design's attitude to transitoriness.

↑	Minor entrance
↗	Meeting room
→	The sunken ground
↪	Aerial view
↳	Entrance courtyard on the east side

Atelier Deshaus   Huaxin Conference Hub   116

Tianlin Road, Xuhui, Shanghai, China

09

2013–2015

↑   Night view of the east entrance

Atelier Deshaus — Huaxin Conference Hub — 118

Tianlin Road, Xuhui, Shanghai, China

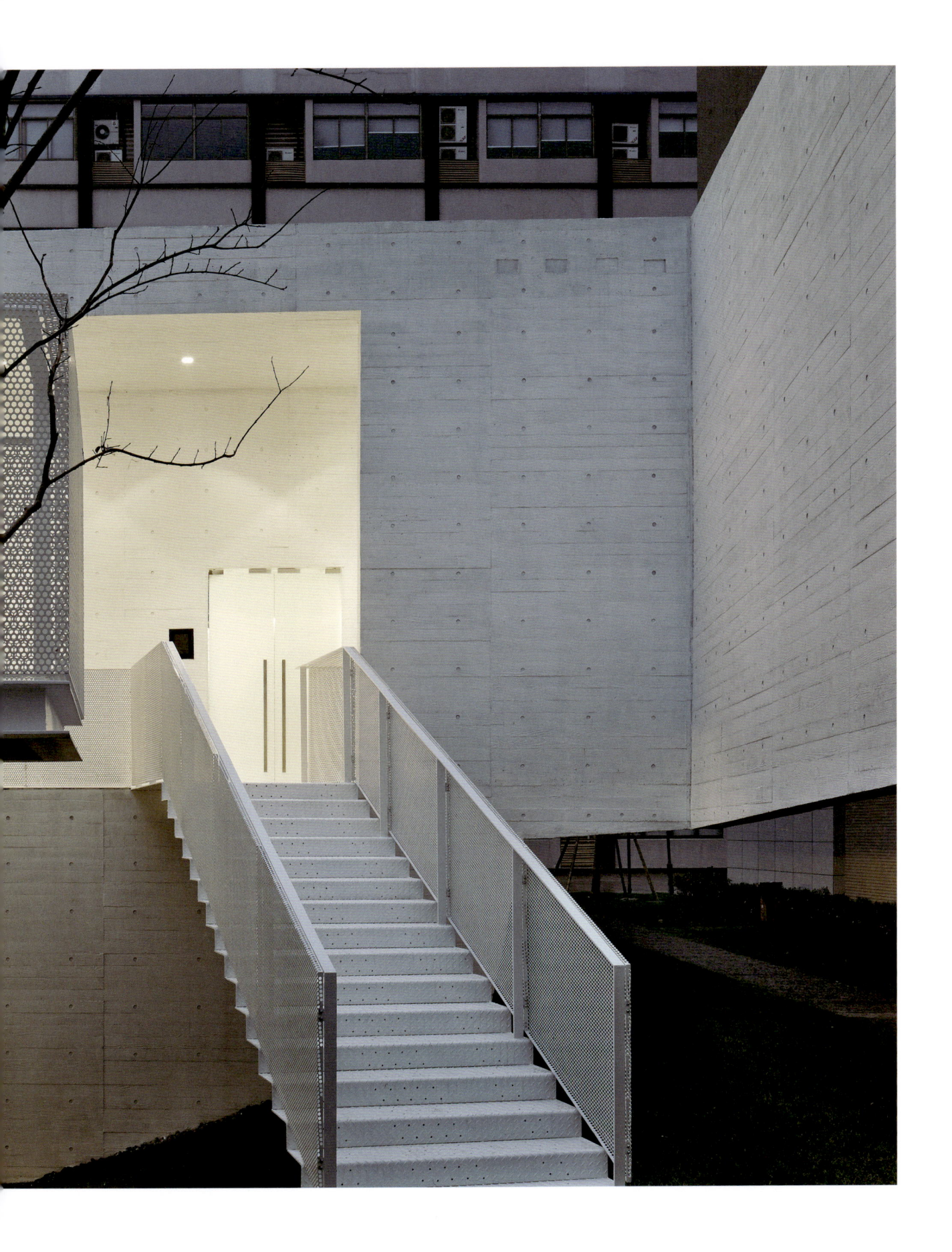

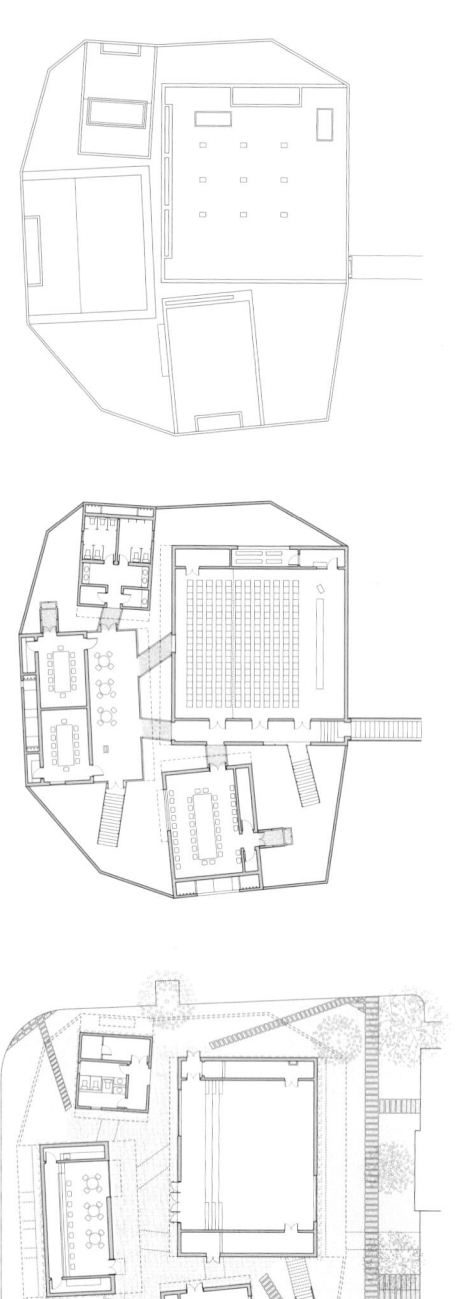

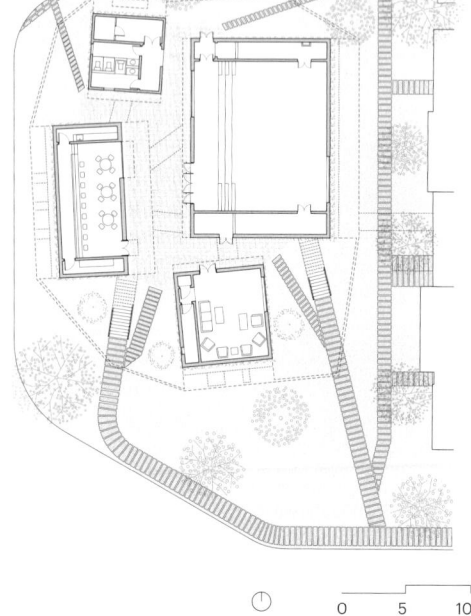

↑   In-between space

↑   First-floor plan
∅   Second-floor plan
↓   Third-floor plan
↪   South elevation
↪   The entrance with elevated walls

0   5   10 m

Atelier Deshaus   Huaxin Conference Hub   120

Tianlin Road, Xuhui, Shanghai, China

10   2014–2017

ONE FOUNDATION KINDERGARTEN IN XINCHANG

Xinchang village in Tianquan County, Sichuan Province
Gross floor area: 1,500 m²

↑   Aerial view

Xinchang village in Tianquan County, Sichuan Province, China

10

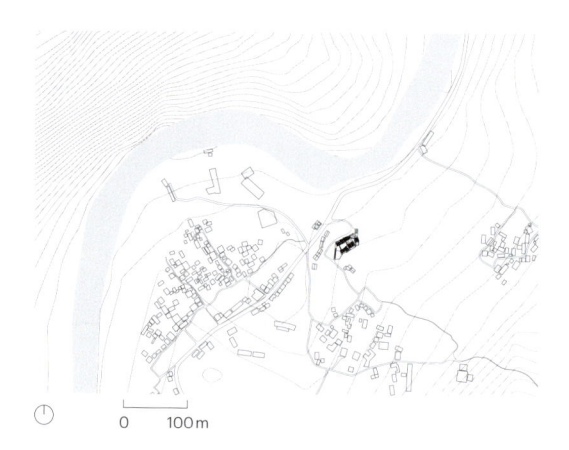

2014–2017

↖ Site plan
↑ View from east

Atelier Deshaus · One Foundation Kindergarten in Xinchang · 124

The kindergarten in Xinchang County has a total of six classes, and is one of more than ten kindergartens to be constructed after the 2013 Lushan earthquake thanks to a donation by One Foundation. The project site is located on a small plateau to the northwest of Ding Village in Xinchang County. Its position, facing a gap in the mountains to the west, means that despite being otherwise surrounded by mountains there is a sense of distance. The nearby villages coexist with nature while also subtly contending with it; an ambience of tranquility prevails.

The entire kindergarten is envisaged as a "village," with a total built area of about 1,500 square meters divided into nine distinct village "cottages" that have different functions. These are placed on the northern, southern, and eastern sides of the site to create a U-shaped courtyard facing the mountain gap to the west. The paving in the courtyard and on the facades uses locally-produced sintered shale bricks, creating a place with a strong sense of artisanry. Consequently, on the one hand the new buildings stand autonomously in the nature that surrounds them, while on the other hand they form an ensemble in conjunction with the sky, the earth, the nearby village, and the mountain gap in the distance. Space and time have their own specified scales here. The manifestations of nature are calibrated and intimately related to the ways in which the site is developed and transformed. The inner courtyard is not only the heart of the kindergarten, but also essential to the locationality and identity of the context. The children will play every day in this courtyard, and so this is where their affinities to and memories of this kindergarten will start. The inner courtyard will thus be the source of the sense of belonging within this context.

The design of the kindergarten also took children's mental and physical attributes into account, integrating spatial types that are as diverse and playful as possible. As it often rains in this part of China, the architectural units of the kindergarten and the main entrance are connected by a zigzagging veranda. The veranda also adapts to shifts in the topography of the site by integrating ramps and stairs, adding an intimate layering of scales and spaces between the courtyard and the buildings and offering more options for the children's daily activities. Strict budgeting necessitated a design that would consider local construction and artisanal skills. With an annual rainfall of more than 2,000 millimeters, waterproofing methods largely inform the exterior design. The individual architectural units are not particularly large, with a single-pitched roof that can quickly drain off the rain while also being easy to construct. Shale bricks stacked to the exterior of the main frame structure are used as a waterproofing strategy; this material is also used to construct the local village buildings since shale bricks are more resistant to rain erosion than normal wall coatings. The veranda has a light steel structure that is easily manually transported to the construction site. This also adds an industrialized product to the artisanry of the shale masonry, thereby distinguishing the architecture of the kindergarten from the buildings in the villages.

Xinchang village in Tianquan County, Sichuan Province, China

10

2014–2017

Atelier Deshaus — One Foundation Kindergarten in Xinchang — 126

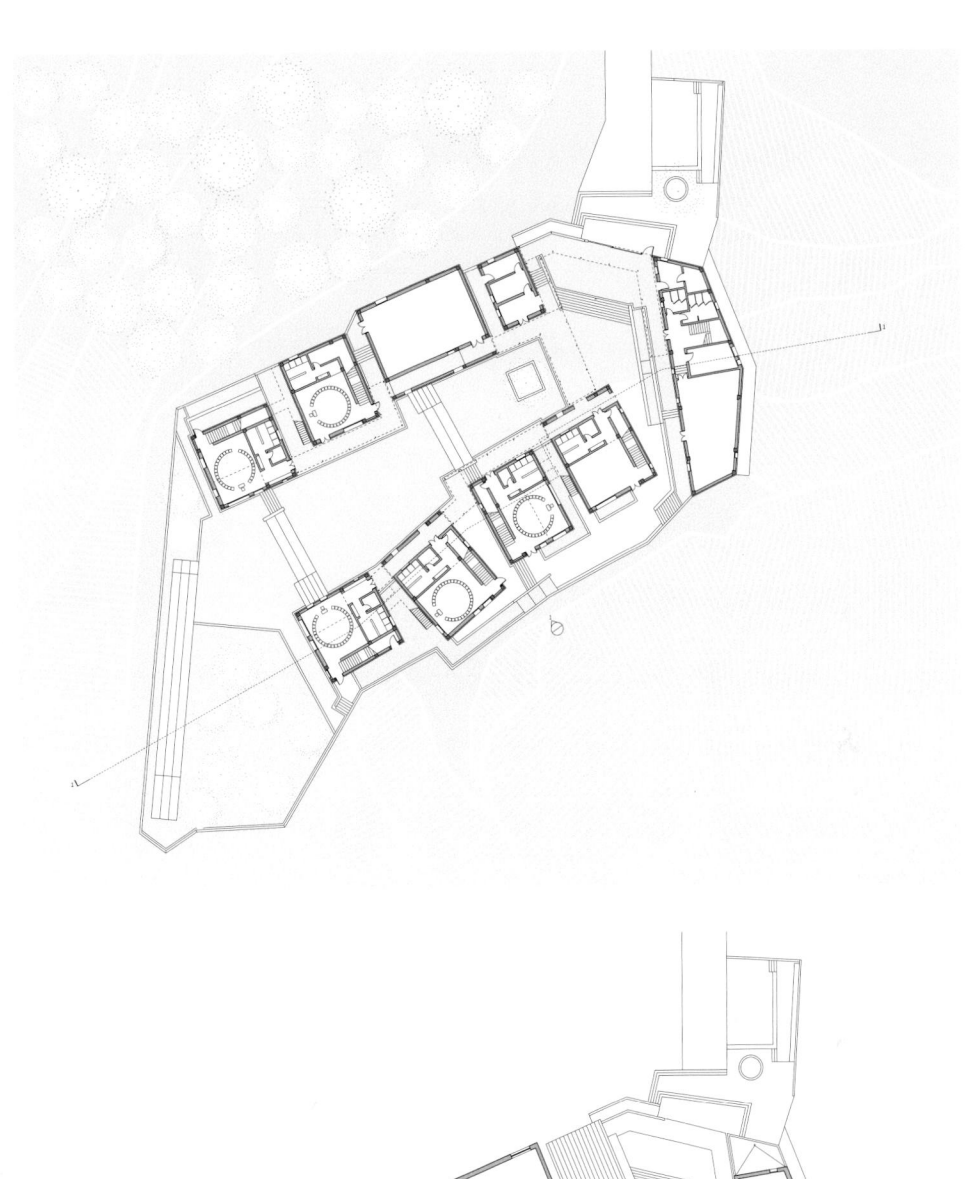

↖ Inner courtyard of the kindergarten
↗ First-floor plan
↘ Second-floor plan

Xinchang village in Tianquan County, Sichuan Province, China

127

↑   View from the courtyard to the mountains

Atelier Deshaus   One Foundation Kindergarten in Xinchang

Xinchang village in Tianquan County, Sichuan Province, China

10

↗ Axonometric diagram   ↪ Site plan
                          ↬ Elevation
                          ↳ Section

Atelier Deshaus   One Foundation Kindergarten in Xinchang   130

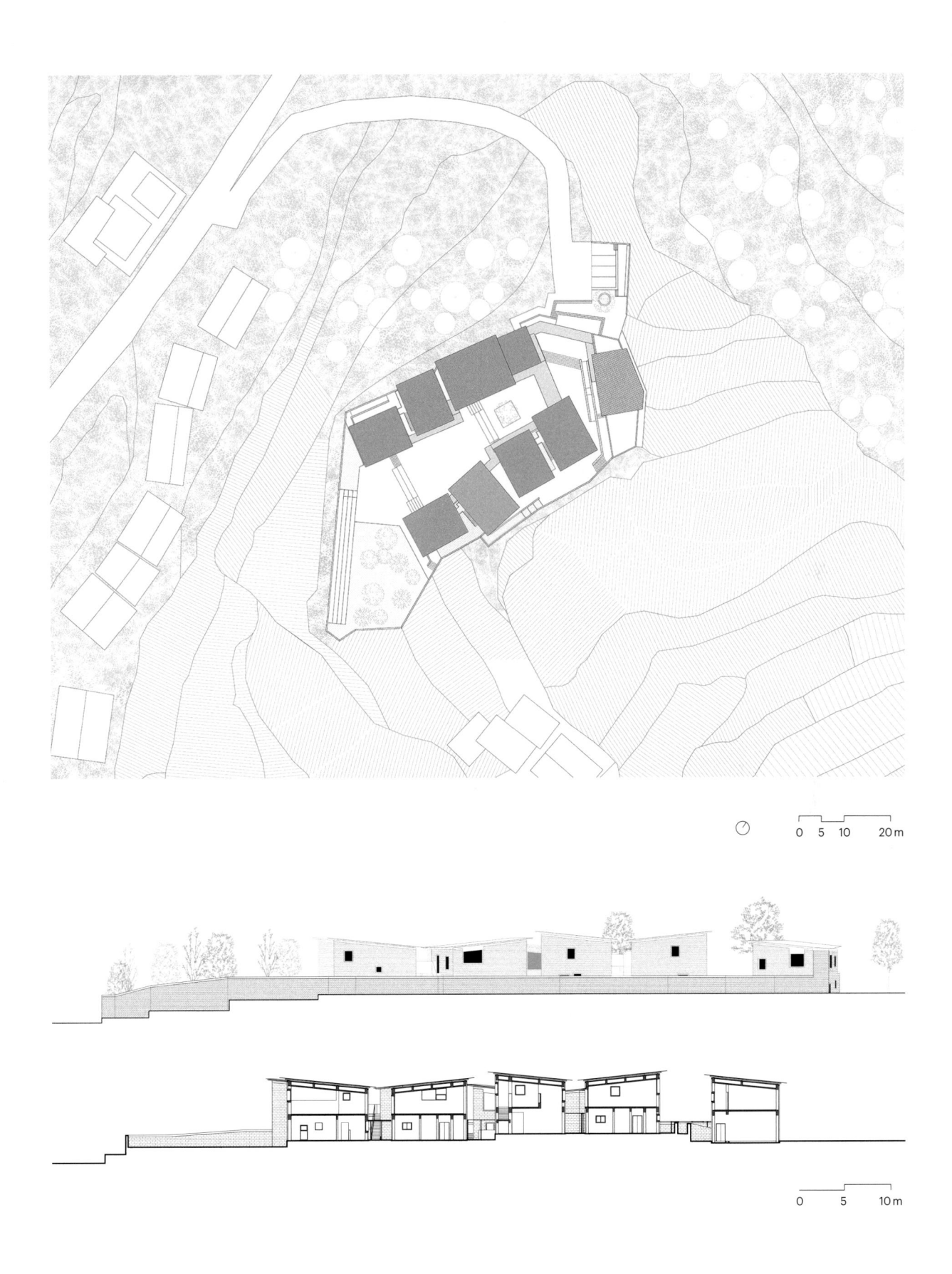

Xinchang village in Tianquan County, Sichuan Province, China

131

↗　　Exterior
→　　Multifunctional room
↬　　The verandas covered with light steel structure
↳　　The veranda space between the walls

Atelier Deshaus　　One Foundation Kindergarten in Xinchang　　132

Xinchang village in Tianquan County, Sichuan Province, China

11   2014–2015
ATELIER DESHAUS OFFICE ON WEST BUND

Longteng Avenue, Xuhui District, Shanghai
Gross floor area: 430 m²

Atelier Deshaus' studio, set on the site of the former Shanghai Aircraft Manufacturing Factory, sits adjacent to a large former industrial hall, which was converted to an interim-use art center, and a cluster of small, pitched-roofed warehouses that were renovated into art studios. Even though the new studio is temporary with a duration of only five years, the design nevertheless reflects the ambience of the industrial site, while requiring a low budget and efficient construction.

The site used to be a concrete parking lot. By using masonry as a structure that could sit on the existing ground as a base, it not only minimizes costs, but also fulfills the needs of a studio with a meeting room, model workshop, office space, storage, and other small-scaled spaces on the ground floor. On the upper floor, a light steel structure spans the open studio space. The layout of work tables of the studio helps determine the spacing of light steel columns and their relation to the windows. Thus, the spatial elements of function are embedded in the logic of the structure, which also reflects in turn the temperament of the industrial site. By placing the light steel columns between windows, the gesture not only imparts on the windows with the duty of preventing thermal bridges, but also allows the structural framework to be clearly read in the interior.

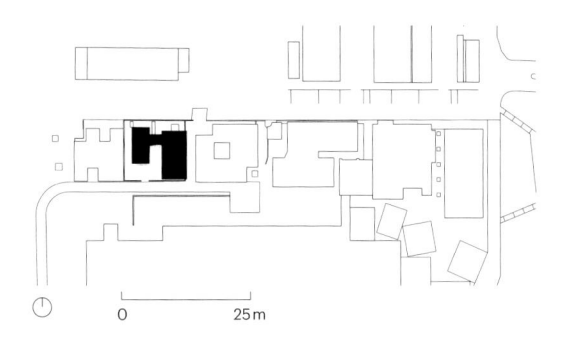

↖   Site plan
↪   Roof terrace

Xuhui District, Shanghai, China

11

2014–2015

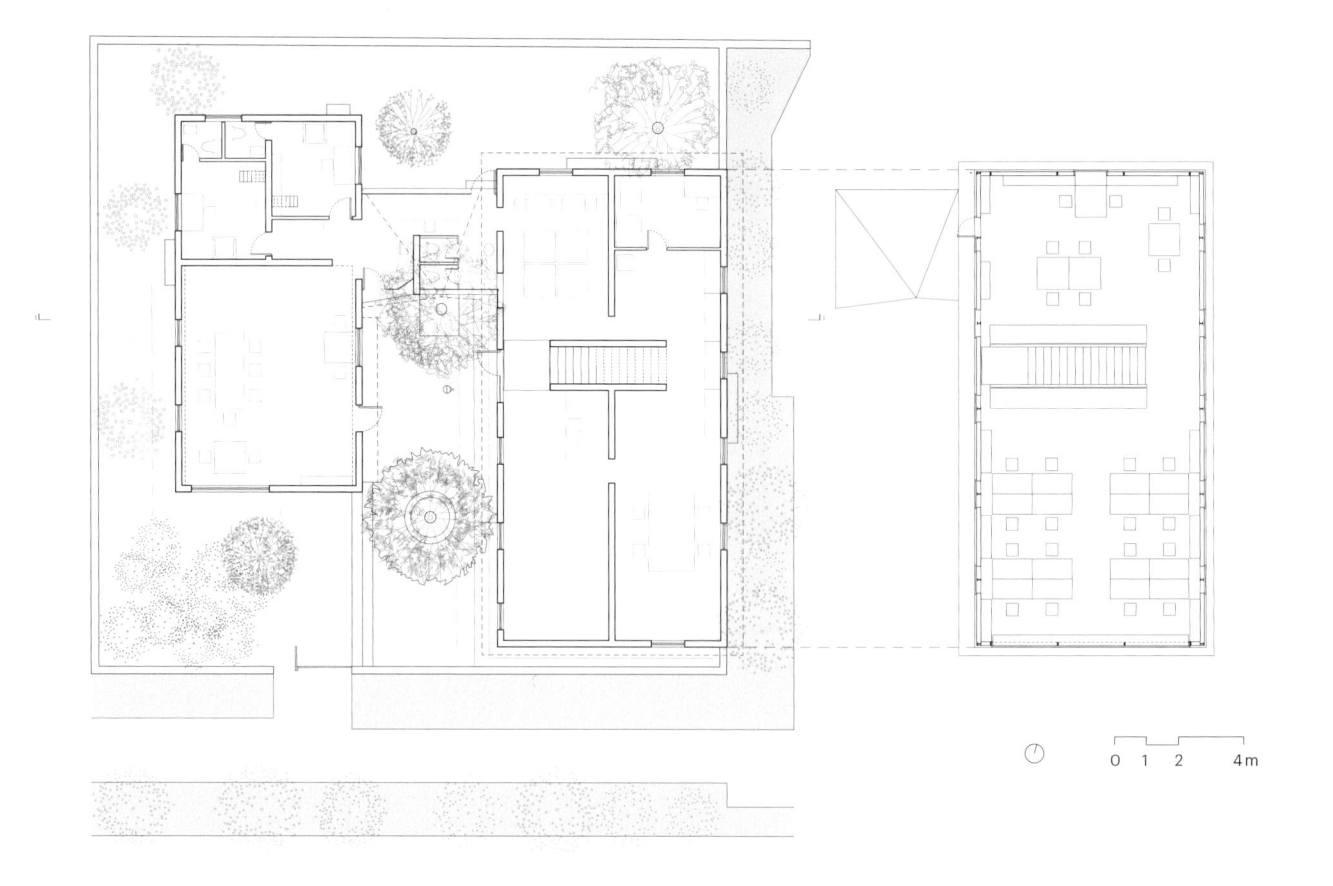

Atelier Deshaus — Atelier Deshaus Office on West Bund — 136

← Model
← Plan of the first and second floors
↑ Space for discussions
→ Workspace

↑ Looking into the meeting room from the front yard

Atelier Deshaus   Atelier Deshaus Office on West Bund

Xuhui District, Shanghai, China

11

2014–2015

Atelier Deshaus Atelier Deshaus Office on West Bund 140

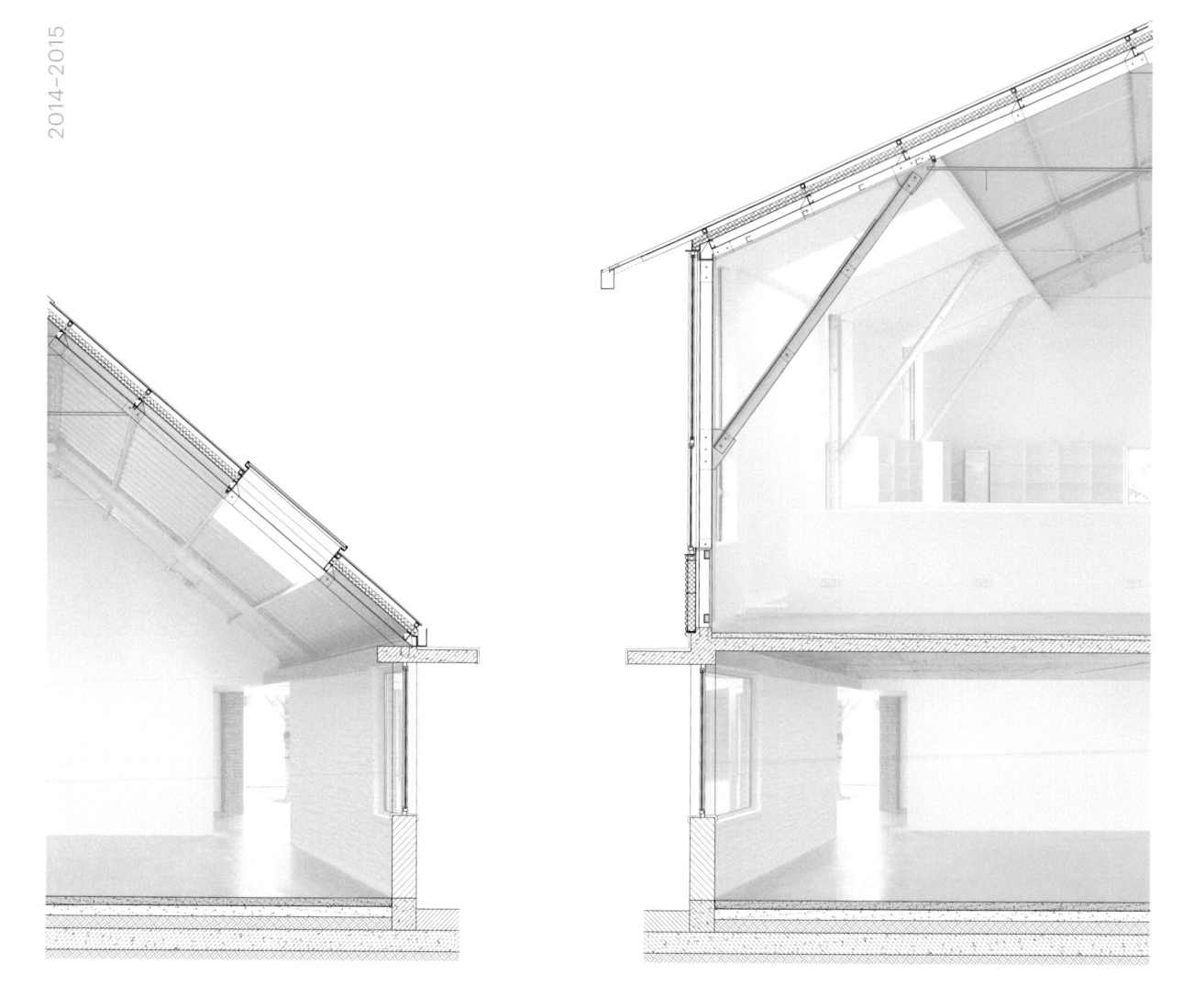

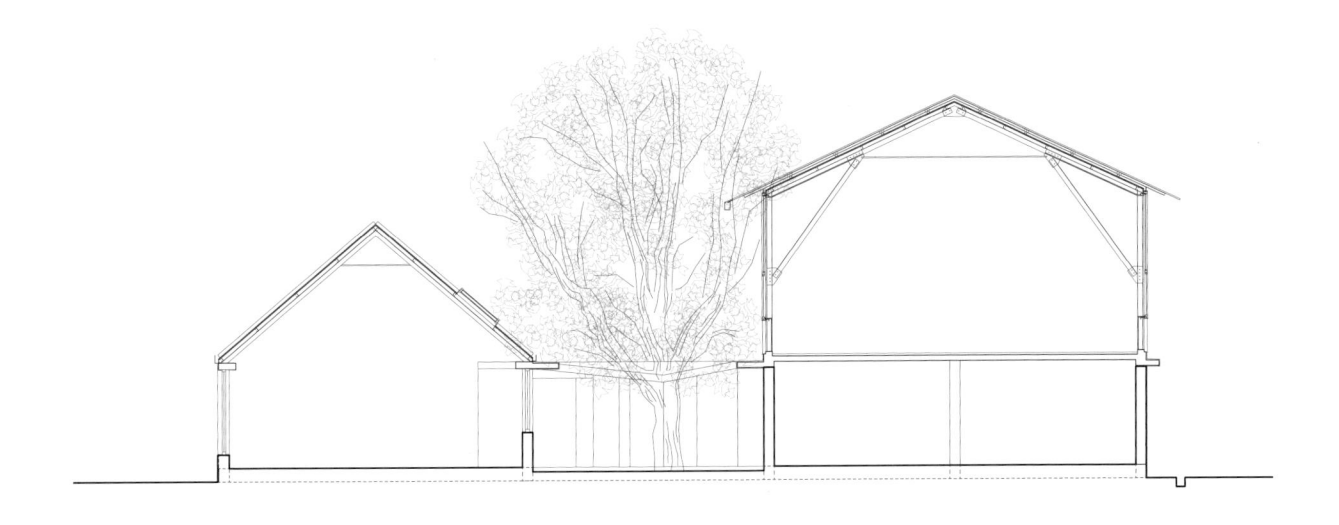

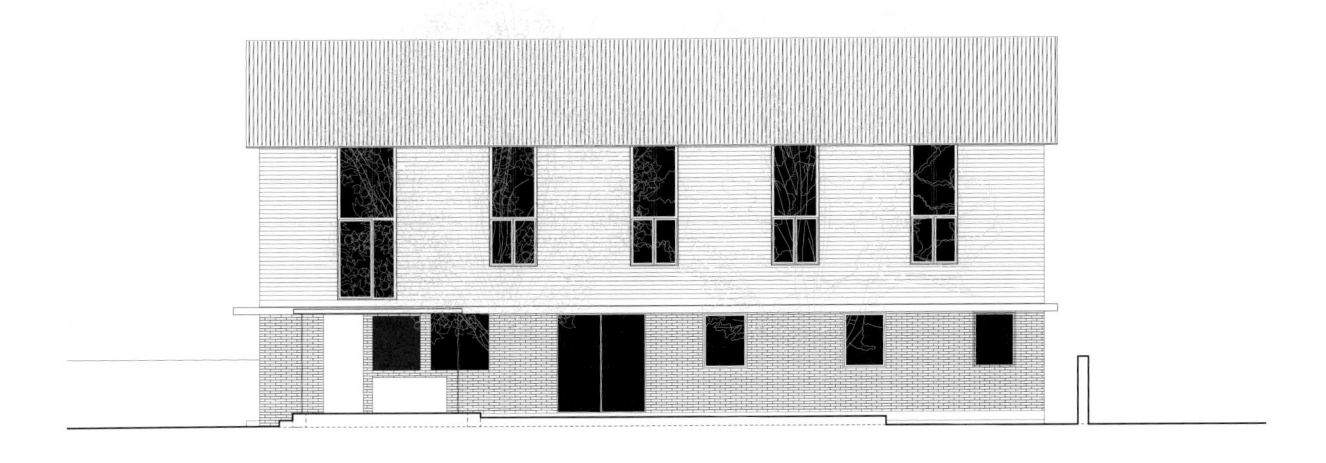

← Model
↵ Section perspective
↑ Section
↓ West elevation

0 1 2   4m

Xuhui District, Shanghai, China

141

12   2015–2019
YUNYANG RIVERFRONT VISITOR CENTER

Binjiang Avenue, Yunyang, Chongqing
Area: 9,011 m²

Located in the region of the Three Gorges Dam, the site in Yunyang in the greenbelt along the Yangtze River is planned for a tourist service center, providing commercial services to residents who visit for leisure. The client wanted to use reclaimed land in a small bay as the site for the future tourist center, which was planned as a two-story building facing the river's flow. During the first site visit when water was collected for the reservoir and the river was almost at its highest level, it was discovered that a natural cliff, falling straight down into water, begins downstream, extends upstream, and comes to a sudden stop after enclosing a half of the bay. Upstream from the bay, the water's edge is sloped and was transformed into an engineered embankment and revetment. Compared to the broad and open surface of the river, the bay and the cliff overgrown with vegetation that exudes serenity and profoundness are in themselves a distinct landscape resource, and thus warrant preserving. The client was persuaded to shift the project site to the upstream side of the bay, allowing the tourist center to be a finish to the new embankment, as well as continuing the cliff, completing the encirclement of the bay, and extending onto the revetment of the river.

↖ Site plan
↦ View from the river

Binjiang Avenue, Yunyang, Chongqing, China

12

↑ The upper-level plaza pointing towards the mountains
↦ Aerial view

Binjiang Avenue, Yunyang, Chongqing, China

↑   The lower-level plaza presenting a huge opening on the elevation

Atelier Deshaus — Yunyang Riverfront Visitor Center

Binjiang Avenue, Yunyang, Chongqing, China

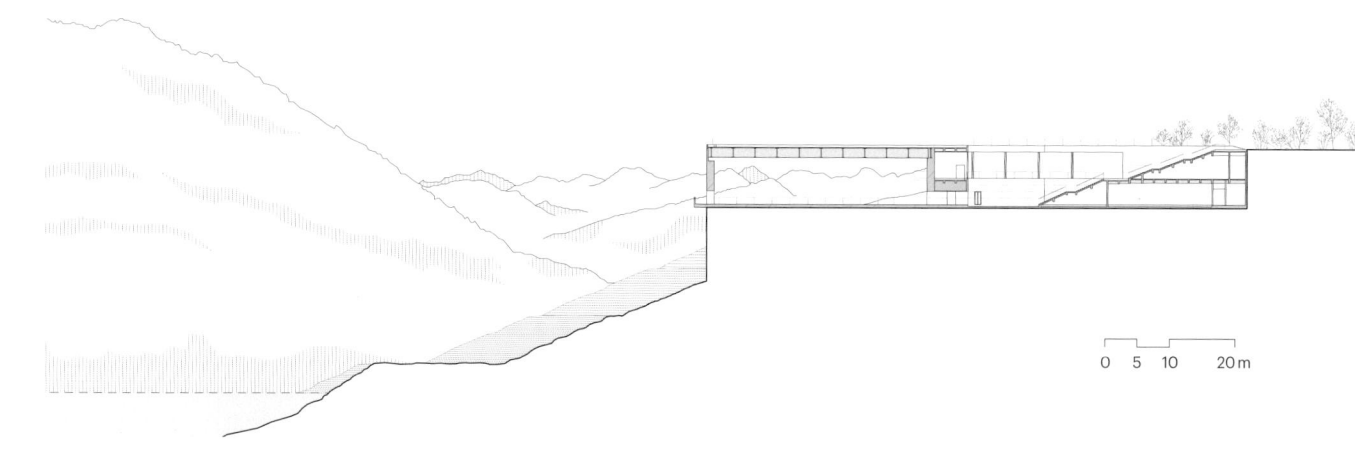

Yunyang is a city in the mountains with a fairly high density. Along the riverside, where there is seldom flat land, roads and greenbelts are located ten to twenty meters above the maximum water level of the Yangtze River. In the design proposal, the tourist center not only fulfills commercial functions, but also can become a place for the local residents' everyday activities, such as outdoor plaza dancing, and also becomes a destination for enjoying the river view. A waterfront plaza is located facing the river, at the same height as the embankment of 1.5 meters above the maximum water level, and close to the water. In order to also give visitors a sense of security so close to the sublime river gorge, the plaza is covered like an over-scaled canopy protecting the people underneath. The waterfront plaza's elevation above the water provides a new viewing perspective for visitors enjoying the river view, who can look up and downstream as well as into the far distance, perceiving the poetic sensation of "river waters gush and flow beyond the horizon [江流天地外]," which contrasts with the usual views across the river. The canopy and its supporting structures frame the view, cropping out the sky, thus highlighting the river and mountains and underlining the sublime of the landscape. With a height difference of nearly ten meters between the waterfront plaza and the riverside roads, they are connected by a grand staircase, on the two sides of which are placed commercial spaces. The roof of the commercial spaces extend into the canopy of the waterfront plaza, creating a platform above that offers another space for the activities of the visitors. In contrast to the canopied plaza, the roof platform is even higher than the embankment, where the experience of the grand universe above and surging river down below is even more magnified.

In some senses, a manmade city in the mountains is the opposite of the river gorges formed by nature. The tourist center situated here is between these oppositions. On the one hand, the architecture corroborates and magnifies the potentials of nature by continuing the cliff, re-enclosing the bay, and completing the new embankment, thus embedding itself in nature. On the other hand, facilitated by elements such as waterfront plaza, the grand staircase and platform, the architecture offers the visitors new possibilities. In connecting the river, the city and people, the tourist service center also achieves its own being.

↑ Section

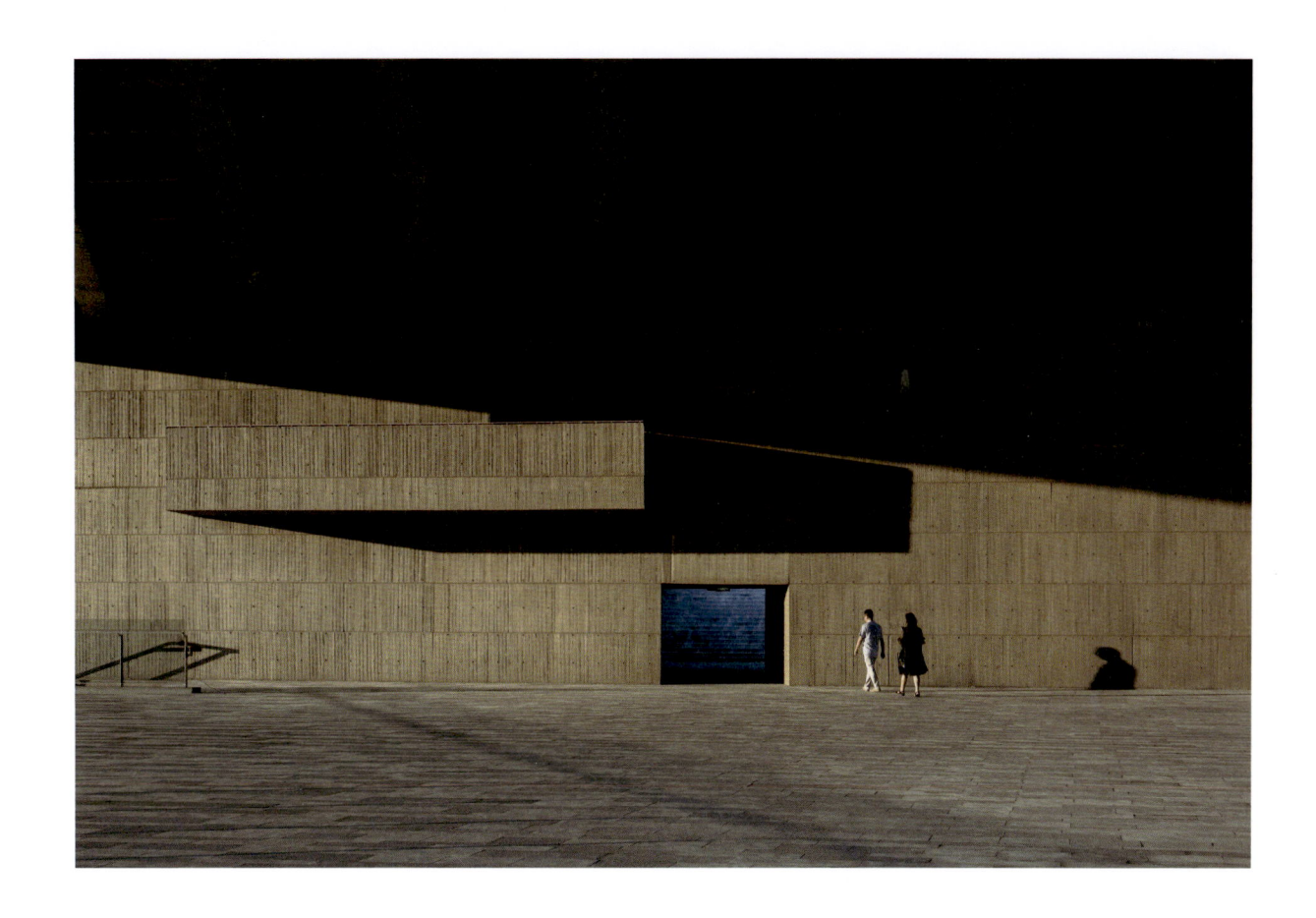

↑ Looking back at the corridor connecting the lower-level plaza and the staircase

↑ Juxtaposition of the visitor center and the cliff

Binjiang Avenue, Yunyang, Chongqing, China

12

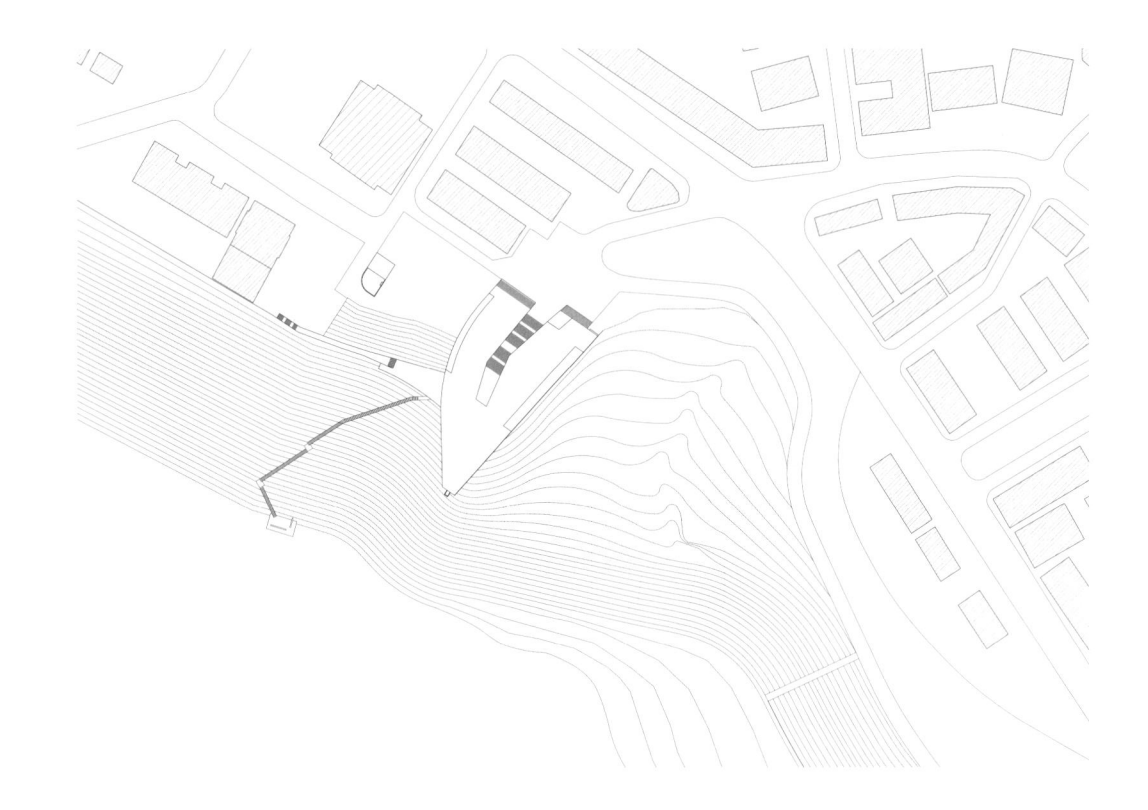

2015–2019

↗ Site plan
→ B2 floor plan
↳ B1 floor plan

0　25　50m

Atelier Deshaus　　Yunyang Riverfront Visitor Center　　150

Binjiang Avenue, Yunyang, Chongqing, China

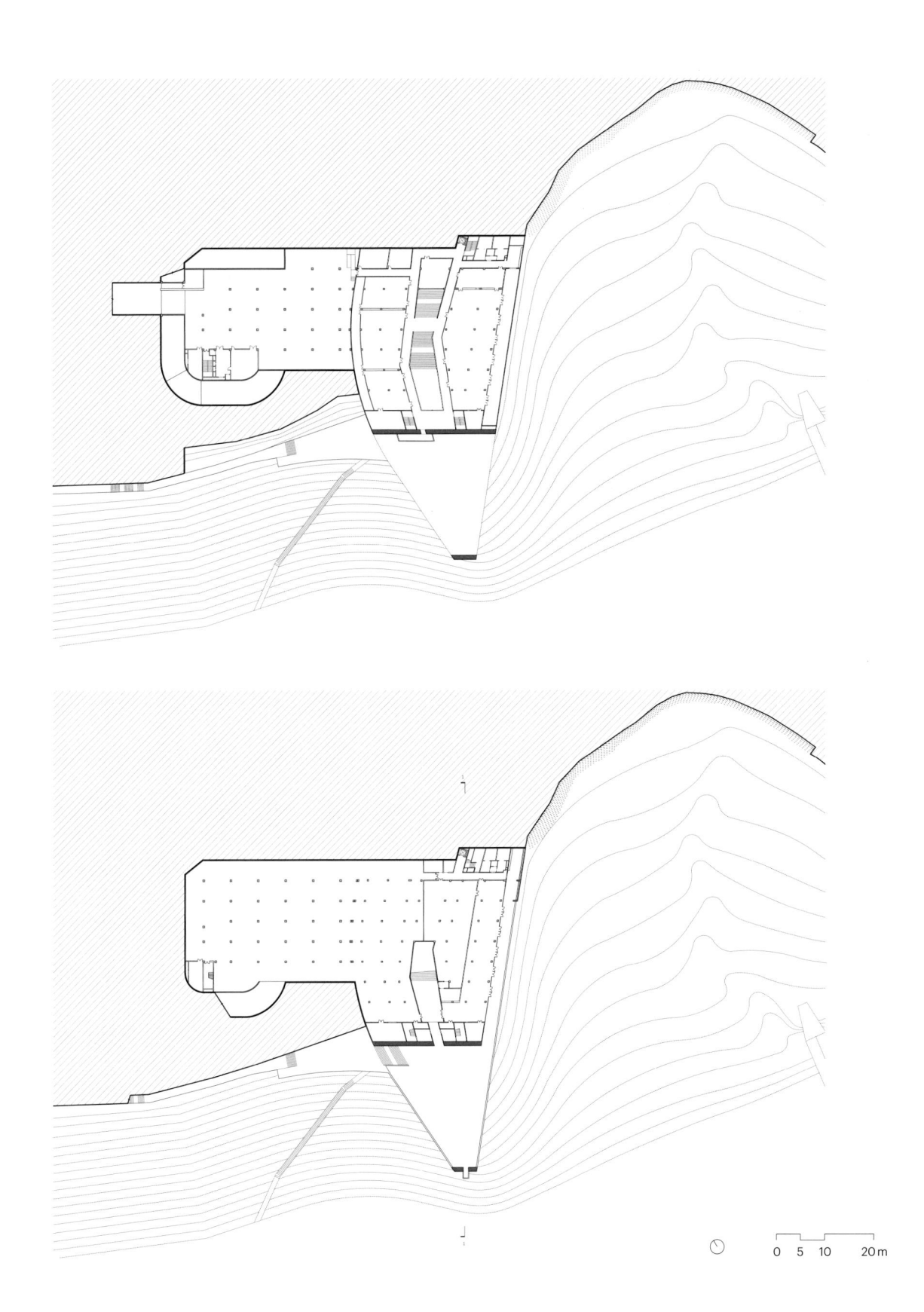

↑ The covered lower-level plaza framing the landscape

Binjiang Avenue, Yunyang, Chongqing, China

13   2015

BLOSSOM PAVILION

West Huaihai Road, Shanghai
Gross floor area: 96 m²

The Blossom Pavilion is a collaboration with the artist Zhan Wang, whose representative sculptures are "scholar rocks" from Lake Tai made of mirror-finish stainless steel. The texture of the sculptures' surface was created by crafting the satin steel directly onto the natural stones. The artist views the Chinese scholar rock as a material object, in contrast to the way it is understood in the traditional Chinese garden, where it is a corporeal embodiment rather than an object to be beheld.

Structure and enclosure are humanity's most basic and primitive spatial construction practices, providing shelter from the sun and rain. As construction evolved, a preference emerged for rationality and scientific laws, underpinned by engineering technologies. The Blossom Pavilion, likewise, underwent rigorous structural calculations. The 12-by-8-meter canopy is made of 8- and 14-millimeter-thick steel plates set within an 800-by-800-millimeter grid, their placing determined by load distribution. Above the plates there are 14-millimeter-thick cloud-shaped ribs, the heights of which vary from 50 to 200 millimeters. The spacing between the ribs is used as flower beds, and thus the structural form becomes a natural topographical slope. Below the plates, six 60-millimeter-diameter square hollow columns or A-shaped steel columns with a solid core are placed according to spatial needs, completing the structure with an austere touch.

↦   Model
↑   *Artifical Rock No.1* by Zhan Wang

Nevertheless, the decisions regarding the location of the supports depend on more than just structural efficiency. In fact, working with the location of the "sliced" scholar rocks allows the supporting structure to start demarcating space, too. By decomposing and transforming the artist's stainless-steel sculptures, the architect is able to create an abstract space that resembles a scholar rock. The surface made from an imprinted stone texture is placed on one side of the "sliced" supports. The opposite surface retains the mirror-finish of the stainless steel. The surrounding trees and greenery are thus integrated into the Blossom Pavilion via the blurred reflections.

Thus, in this manner, the artist has made it possible for the architect to experiment with the rhetoric of primitive space.

Atelier Deshaus — Blossom Pavilion — 156

← Inner reflection
↗ Aerial view

13

2015

0 1 2 4m

↑ First-floor plan
↓ Structural axonometric diagram

↱ View from outside
↳ View from inside

Atelier Deshaus · Blossom Pavilion · 158

West Huaihai Road, Shanghai, China

↑ The cantilevered space

West Huaihai Road, Shanghai, China

14   2015–2019

TAIZHOU CONTEMPORARY ART MUSEUM

Shameng Food Warehouse, Fengshan Road,
Jiaojiang District, Taizhou, Zhejiang
Gross floor area: 2,454 m^2

Taizhou Contemporary Art Museum is located inside a cultural and creative park that was converted from a former grain storage facility. The compound includes a number of factory buildings and warehouses in the Soviet style that have been converted into shops, restaurants, and offices. Although the renovated park is full of life, the feeling of the original grain store has not been well preserved. The museum is a new build on a vacant site in the compound, facing a small plaza. From the site it is possible to see the continuous Feng Mountains to the east behind a row of two-story buildings.

With a total floor area of 2,454 square meters, the museum has eight exhibition spaces. As each of these exhibition areas is quite small, high-ceilinged, interlocking levels decrease the overall height from the lower halls to the upper ones, while also modifying the rhythm of the promenade. The spatial overlaps of the exhibition spaces on different levels create a dynamic spatial sequence as well as a rich experience for museum visitors.

The museum's barrel-vault cast-in-situ concrete ceiling creates a unique ambience. The linear barrel-vaulted structure not only accommodates the exhibition lighting system but also links the interior and exterior of the building. In terms of spatial sequence, the exhibition space begins on the first floor where it opens toward the plaza, as suggested by the orientation of the barrel vault. It then ascends and turns before finally culminating in the uppermost exhibition hall, where it opens up once again, this time toward Feng Mountain. The top barrel vault is also turned in this direction, shaping a dialogue between structure and landscape. Similarly, the southern facade of the museum is composed of concave curves, which seem to be extending the inner barrel-vaulted structure and presenting a front view of the museum to the plaza.

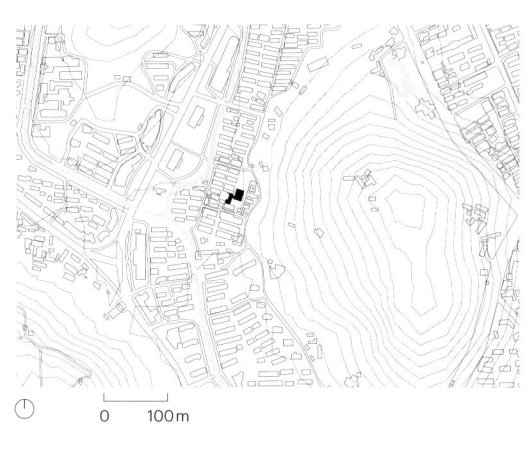

↖   Site plan
↦   Concrete space

Jiaojiang District, Taizhou, Zhejiang, China

↑   The exhibition hall on the top floor opening up onto the mountains

Jiaojiang District, Taizhou, Zhejiang, China

↗   Detail   ↪   Detail

Atelier Deshaus   Taizhou Contemporary Art Museum   166

The rough surface incorporates all the inaccuracies and errors that came from the concrete being badly poured in-situ, but this actually resulted in an undesigned expressiveness. Throughout construction, door and window fixtures as well as interior design strategies had to be constantly adjusted on site to fit the changing conditions, in order to turn the inadvertent, ruin-like crudeness into an exquisite spatial quality.

Jiaojiang District, Taizhou, Zhejiang, China

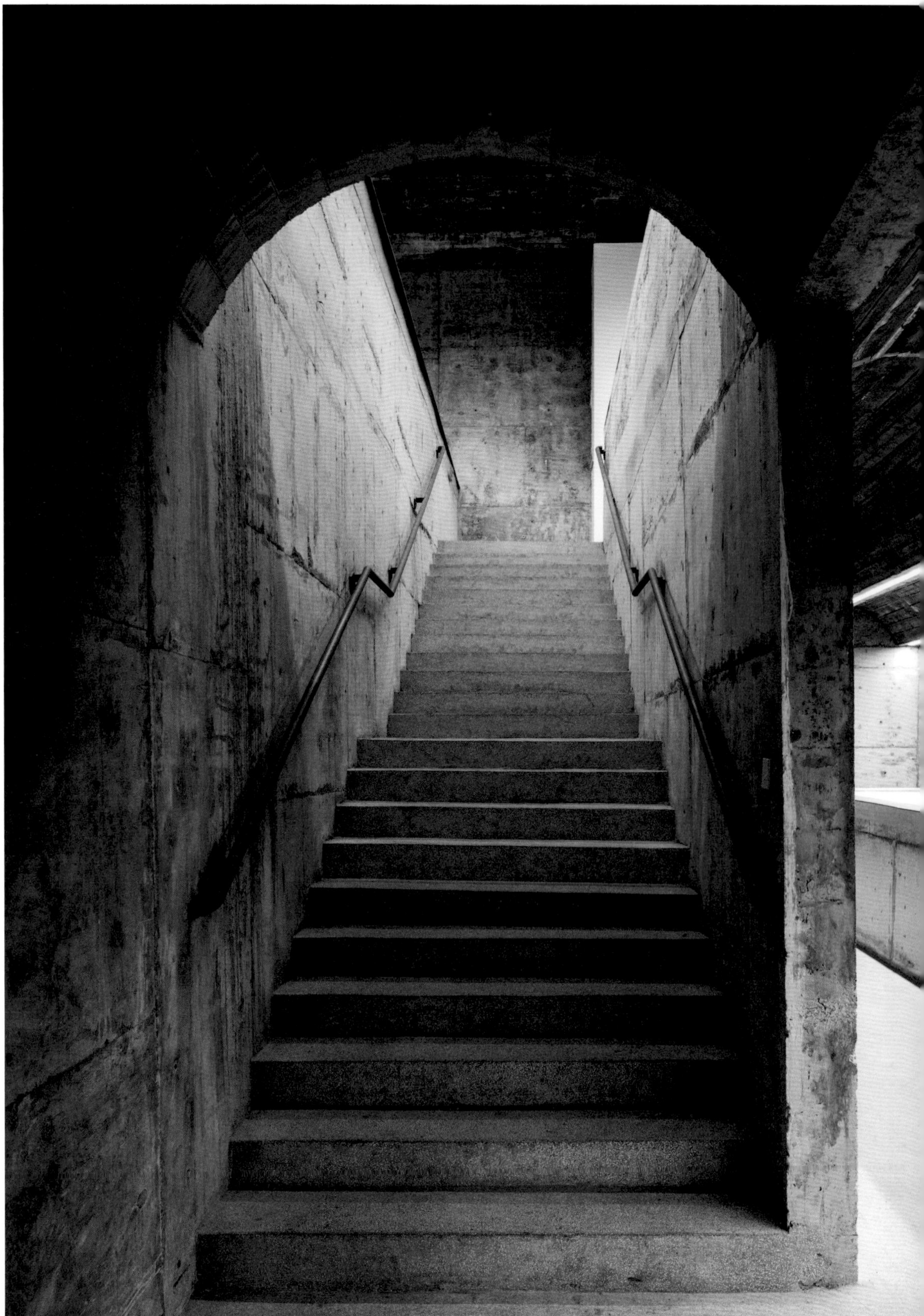

↖ The staircase
↑ Exhibition hall covered with plasterboard
↓ Continuous vault

Jiaojiang District, Taizhou, Zhejiang, China

169

14

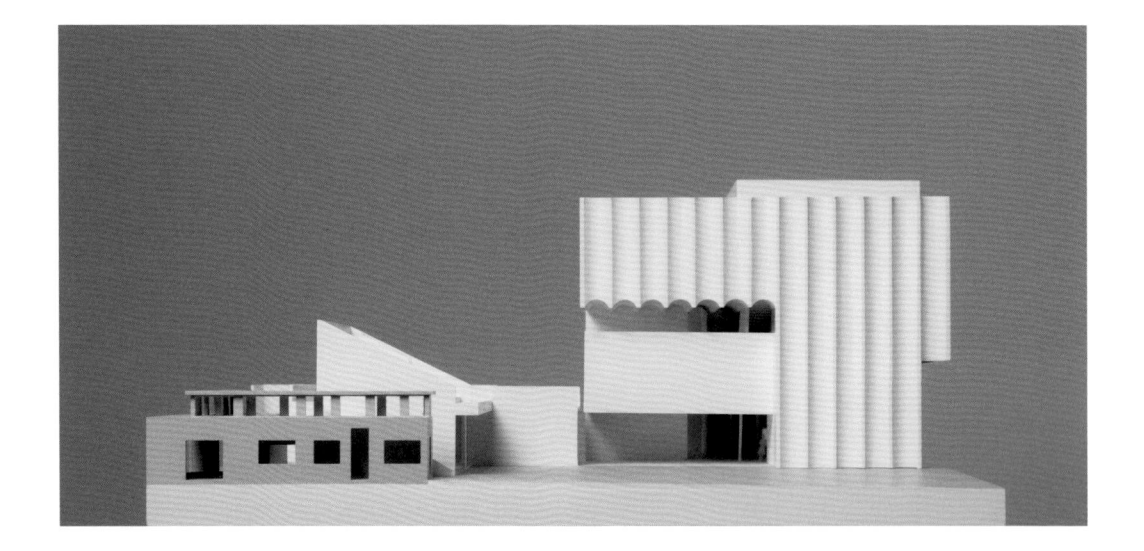

2015–2019

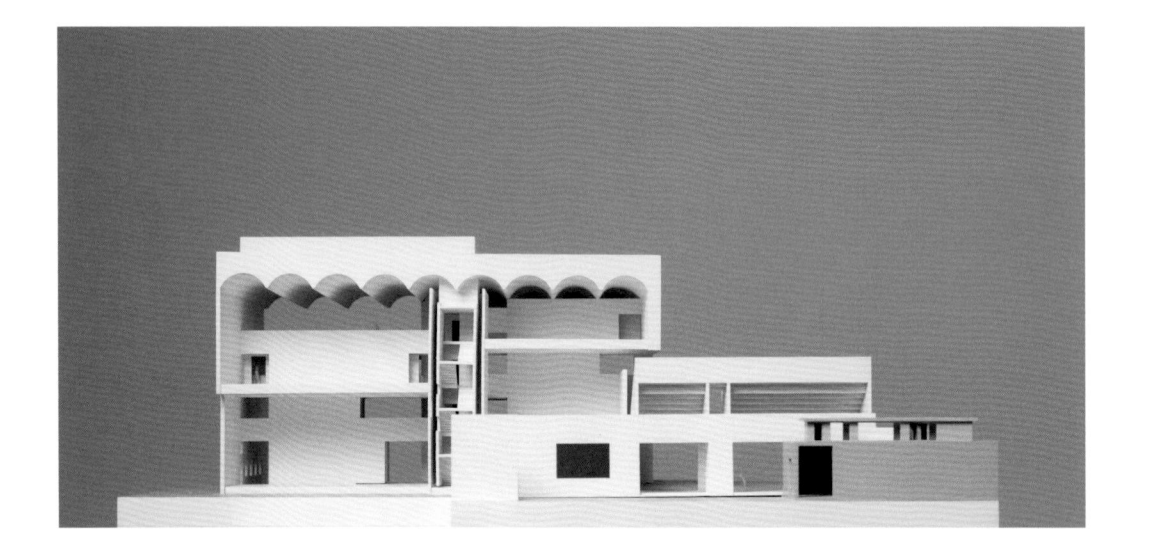

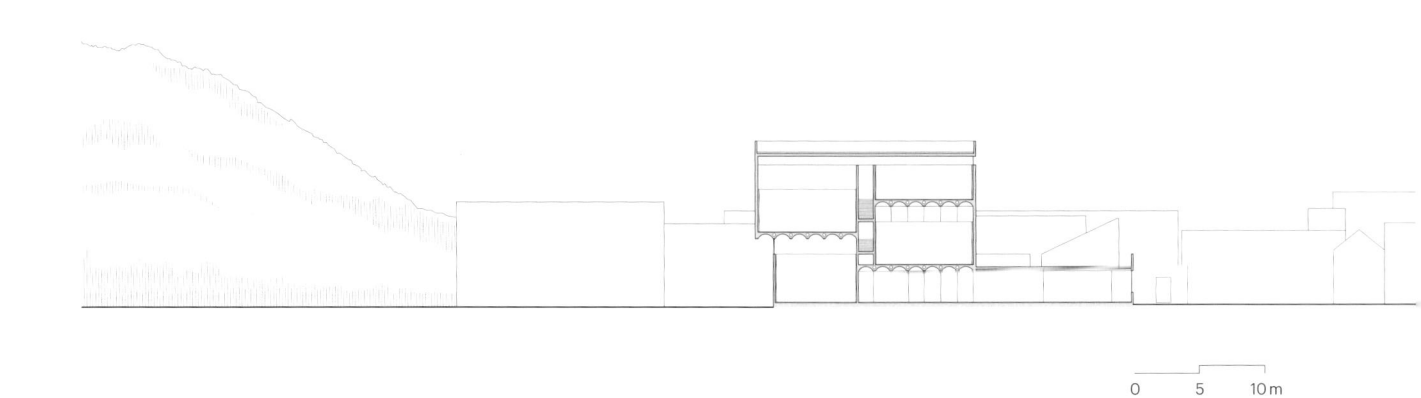

0   5   10 m

Atelier Deshaus   Taizhou Contemporary Art Museum   170

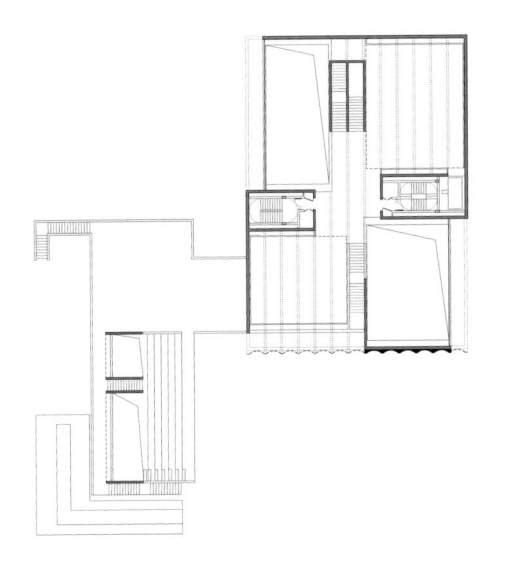

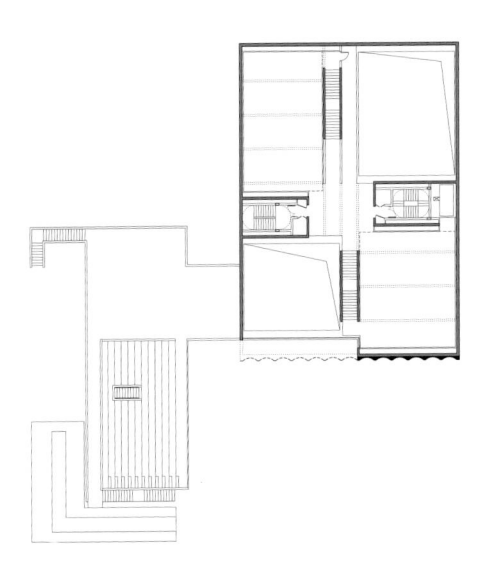

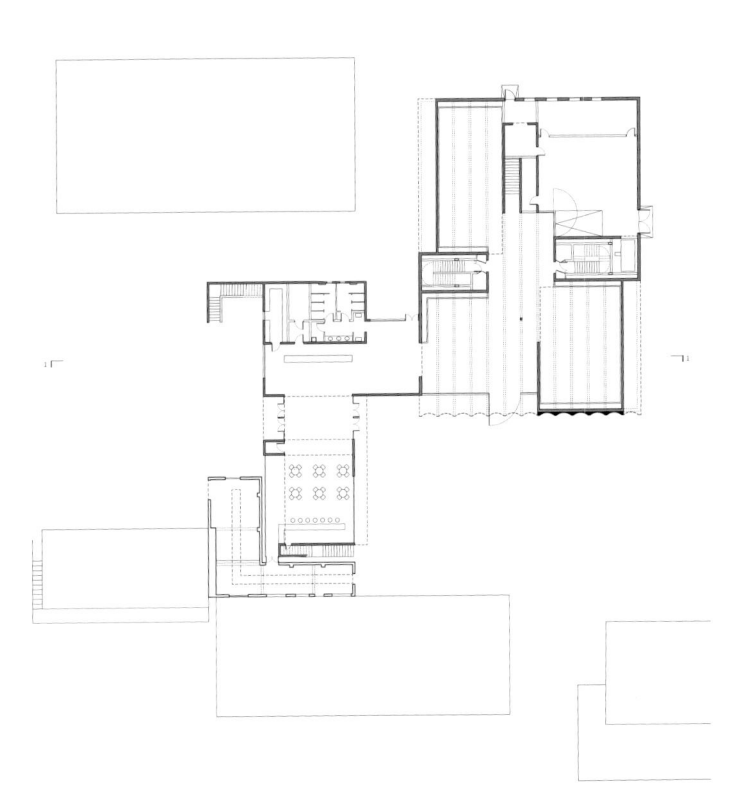

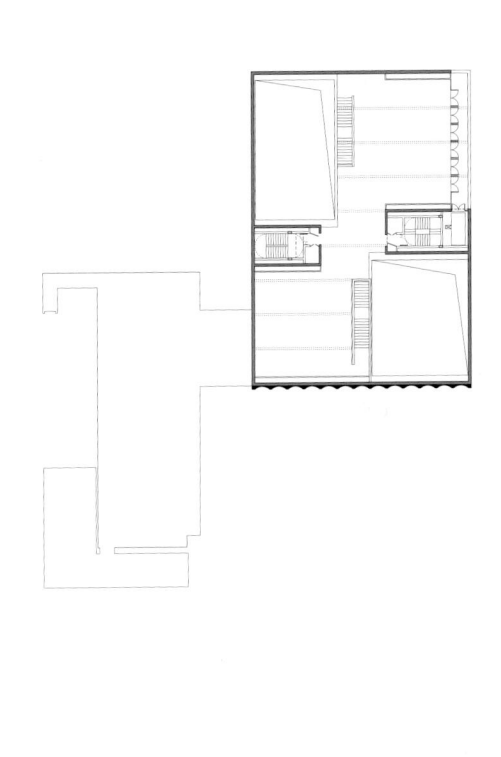

← Model
← Model Section
← Section

↖ First-floor plan
↗ Second-floor plan
↙ Third-floor plan
↘ Fourth-floor plan

0 5 10 m

Jiaojiang District, Taizhou, Zhejiang, China

171

↗ Monumentality of the museum → Opening in the exhibition hall on the top floor
↳ Museum and part of the plaza

Atelier Deshaus — Taizhou Contemporary Art Museum

Jiaojiang District, Taizhou, Zhejiang, China

↑ View towards the museum from the alley

Jiaojiang District, Taizhou, Zhejiang, China

15   2015–2016

MODERN ART MUSEUM SHANGHAI AND ITS WALKWAYS

Waterfront of Laobaidu Wharf, Pudong, Shanghai
Floor area: around 9,180 m²

The Modern Art Museum in Shanghai is situated on what was once Laobaidu Coal Wharf in the city's Pudong district. Almost all of the coal storage infrastructure had been demolished, but some of the temporary exhibitions that the architect organized amongst the ruins persuaded the client to preserve the remaining infrastructure. A suspension structure was designed in order to optimize the organization of the space while minimizing further damage to the coal infrastructure. This featured a large set of trusses hung from the uppermost columns that remained after the roof was removed. Layering the trusses downwards, the floor slabs were connected to the suspended hooks on one side and to the original structure of the coal bunker on the other side. The design completes the circulation organization while also opening up the view to the scenic Huangpu River, which had been closed off in the former warehouse infrastructure.

The first floor has a multifunctional lobby with eight original coal hoppers forming its ceiling, contrasting the rough exposed infrastructure inside to the polished anodized aluminum cladding on the outside. On the second floor is a compressed multimedia exhibition space partitioned by the slanting surfaces of the coal hoppers. The main exhibition space of the art museum is on the third floor, where the original walls separating the eight coal hoppers were opened to form one unique exhibition space characterized by the rough texture of the original coarse concrete walls. On the fourth floor there is another full-height exhibition space that is directly accessible from the exterior by a grand steel staircase; these stairs have been converted from the old coal-loading channel and offer an alternative circulation route to accommodate the museum's operational activities and exhibitions. The preserved historical structure is not openly displayed on the outside, it is instead concealed in the core of a seemingly brand-new building.

0   100 m

↖   Site plan
↳   View from the river

Atelier Deshaus   Modern Art Museum Shanghai and Its Walkways   176

Waterfront of Laobaidu Wharf, Pudong, Shanghai, China

15

2015–2016

↖ The coal bunker before the renovation
↑ Public platform surrounding the building

Atelier Deshaus	Modern Art Museum Shanghai and Its Walkways	178

↗ Riverfront elevation

Waterfront of Laobaidu Wharf, Pudong, Shanghai, China

↑ The riverside museum and the grand staircase

Waterfront of Laobaidu Wharf, Pudong, Shanghai, China

15

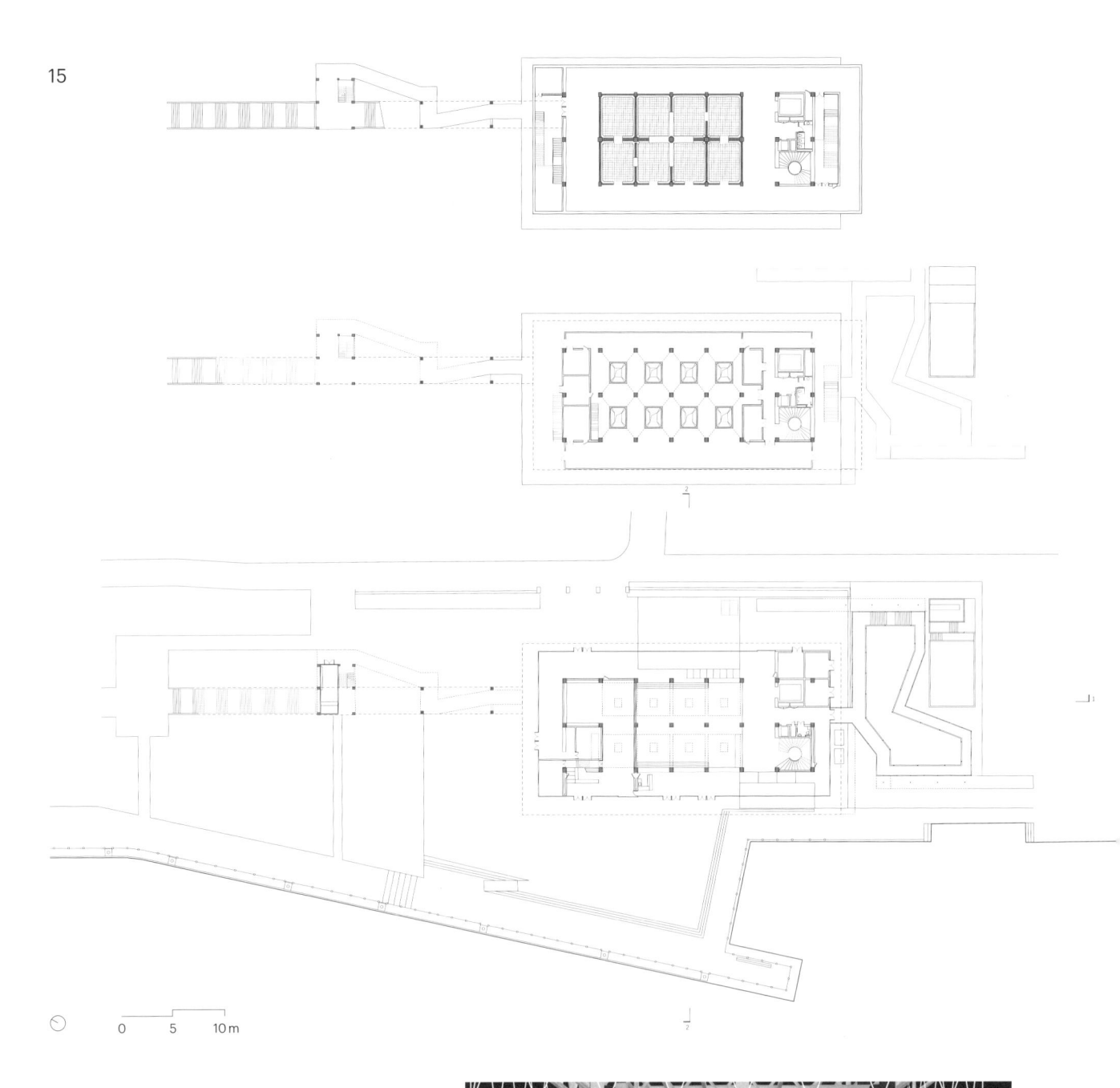

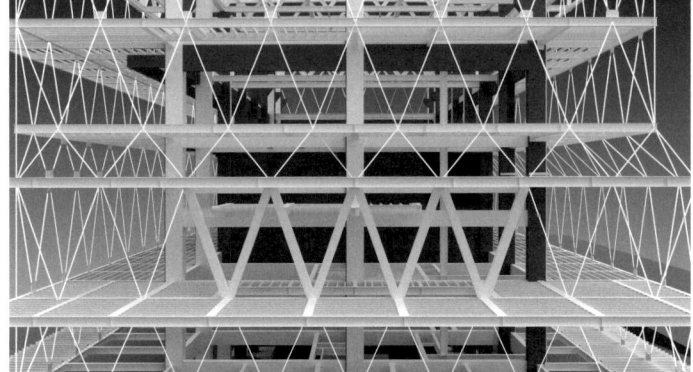

↑ Third-floor plan
↑ Second-floor plan
↗ First-floor plan
→ Structural rendering

Atelier Deshaus   Modern Art Museum Shanghai and Its Walkways   182

↥ Permeable public space
↑ View towards Huangpu River
↓ Section 1–1

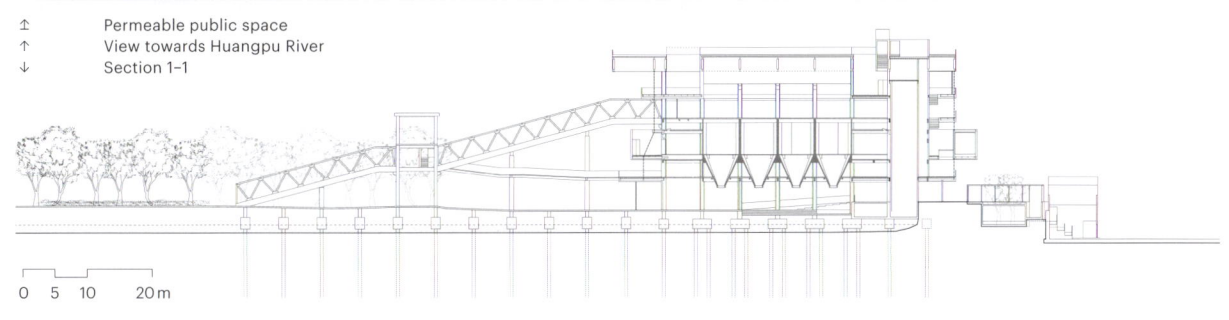

0 5 10   20 m

Waterfront of Laobaidu Wharf, Pudong, Shanghai, China

183

↑ First-floor exhibition hall
↱ Spiral staircase
↦ Renovated coal hopper gallery on the third floor

Waterfront of Laobaidu Wharf, Pudong, Shanghai, China

MUSEUM WALKWAY WITH CAFÉS AND SHOPS
Sited in the Pudong district, the elevated coal-loading channel of Laobaidu Coal Warehouse is approximately 250 meters long. Before the renovation, only rows of parallel concrete frames remained, connected by perpendicular beams at intervals. The newly-built walkway on the coal-loading channel belongs to the Modern Art Museum, but it is also part of the reconstructed urban waterfront public space along the Huangpu River. The upper level is the elevated walkway for pedestrians, while the first-floor level is occupied by art shops and cafés, which contribute to the waterfront public space while also offering potential uses for the museum.

The elevated walkway brings together a new beam string and suspended steel structural system with the existing concrete frames that have weathered on the surface, forming a new structural entity while still maintaining their own visual integrity. This entity both supports the structure of the elevated walkway above and provides a roof for the glass-enclosed shops on the ground. It is a structural plinth that floats the shop volumes within the concrete frames while still being part of the entire structure. Rather than underlining the existing structures on the site, it allows the historic ruin to blend into the new construction, allowing the industrial fragments of the past to remain a subtle part of everyday life in Shanghai.

↑ The coal channels before the renovation

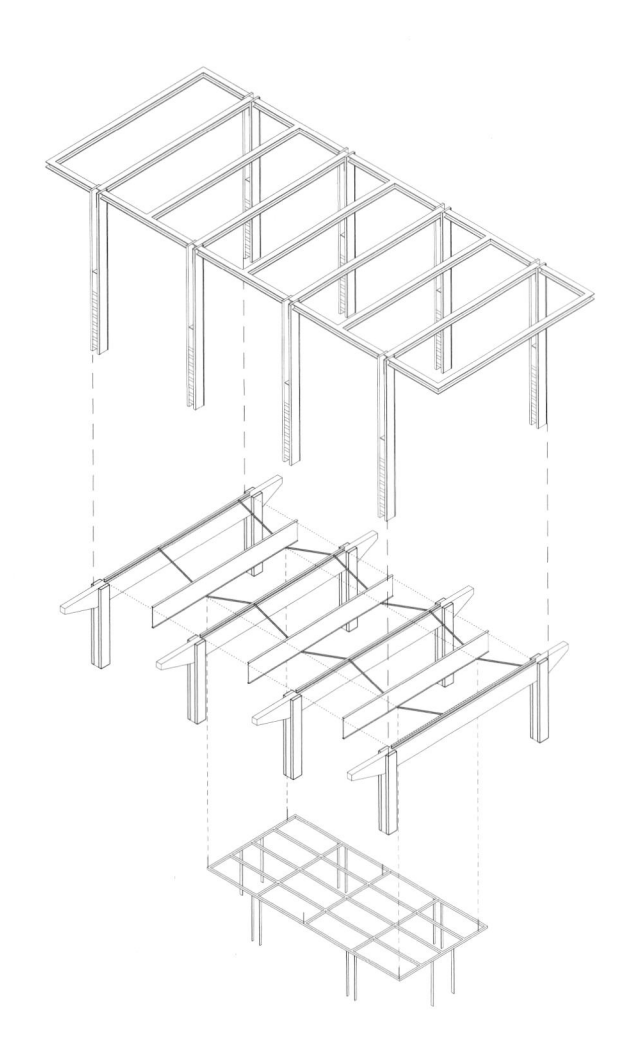

↑ Structural axonometric diagram

Waterfront of Laobaidu Wharf, Pudong, Shanghai, China

↑ The glass boxes of retail spaces under the elevated walkways

Waterfront of Laobaidu Wharf, Pudong, Shanghai, China

15

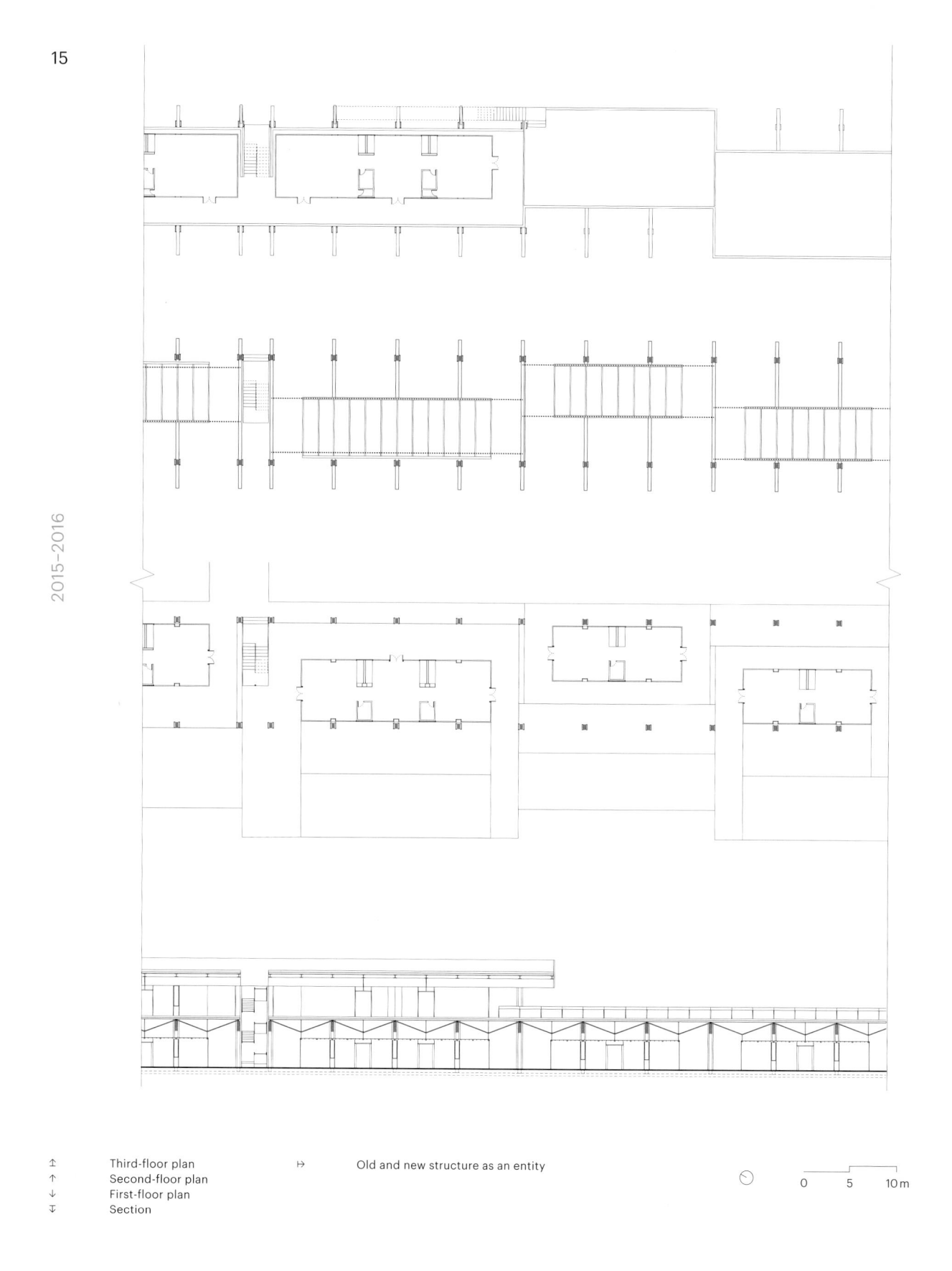

2015–2016

⇕ Third-floor plan
↑ Second-floor plan
↓ First-floor plan
⇳ Section

↦ Old and new structure as an entity

0   5   10 m

Atelier Deshaus	Modern Art Museum Shanghai and Its Walkways	190

Waterfront of Laobaidu Wharf, Pudong, Shanghai, China

15

2015–2016

Atelier Deshaus — Modern Art Museum Shanghai and Its Walkways

← The elevated walkway ↑ New structures upon the old

Waterfront of Laobaidu Wharf, Pudong, Shanghai, China   193

16   2015–2016

TEA HOUSE IN LI GARDEN

Longteng Avenue, Xuhui District, Shanghai
Gross floor area: 19 m²

A tall paulownia tree stands at the corner of a garden that measures approximately 110 square meters, and it is under this tree that the tea house and study is located. The garden also has two staircases, which link the tea house to the meeting room on the second floor and to the client's office on the third floor of the adjacent office building, thereby allowing the tea house to be used both as a private space and as a place for receiving guests.

In order to minimize the impact of the tea house in the small garden, it is located as close as possible to the paulownia tree in the northwest corner. With its crown soaring high in the sky, the paulownia's trunk, with a diameter of 90 centimeters, also becomes a spatial element of the tea house. Together with the back wall, the space behind the tea house is enclosed as part of its interior, thus further reducing the new volume itself.

In order to reduce the footprint of the tea house, a detailed spatial organization of the interior elements and their functions was first produced, resulting in a design of three cantilevered slabs at different heights. The first cantilever is 45 centimeters above the ground, serving as a bench encircling the building. The upper surface of this cantilever is inside while the lower one is outside. On the southern side where it faces the garden, the bench is turned to face the exterior. The second cantilevered slab is placed 1.8 meters above the ground, and expands the interior without limiting one's movement under its exterior eaves. The roof is the third cantilevered slab, defining the different exteriors on the southern, northern, and western sides. While the tea house occupies a footprint of 19 square meters, this roof covers an area of 40 square meters, extending out in different directions to reinforce the spatial relationship between the tea house and the garden.

↖   Site plan
↦   View from afar

Atelier Deshaus   Tea House in Li Garden   194

The square 60-by-60-millimeter steel sections were deliberately chosen as horizontal and vertical structural members because of their slender nature. These sections can be read as part of the structure and as being on the same scale as furniture, thus evoking a domestic resonance with the human body.

The roof is made of 8-millimeter-thick steel plates, with the insulation board fixed by reversed ribbed steel panels to keep the roof smooth. The suspended ceiling used for the lighting system and thermal insulation also hides the structural beams, while the air conditioning is located beneath the floor.

↑   Aerial view

Atelier Deshaus   Tea House in Li Garden

Longteng Avenue, Xuhui, Shanghai, China

16

↑ Partial view of roof structure
↗ View from the paulownia tree towards the tea house
→ Sitting on the bench on the veranda
↪ View from interior towards the main courtyard

Atelier Deshaus Tea House in Li Garden

Longteng Avenue, Xuhui, Shanghai, China

16

2015–2016

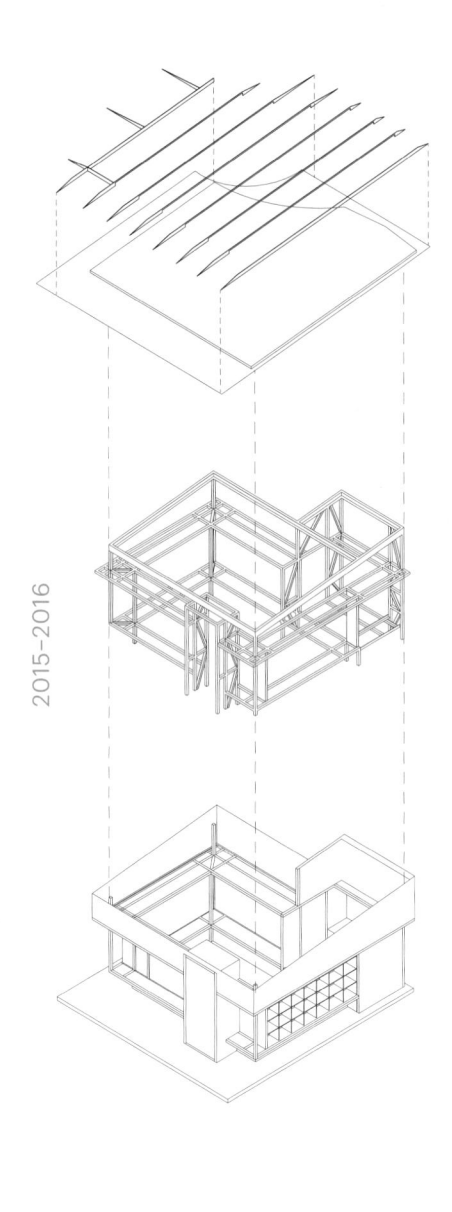

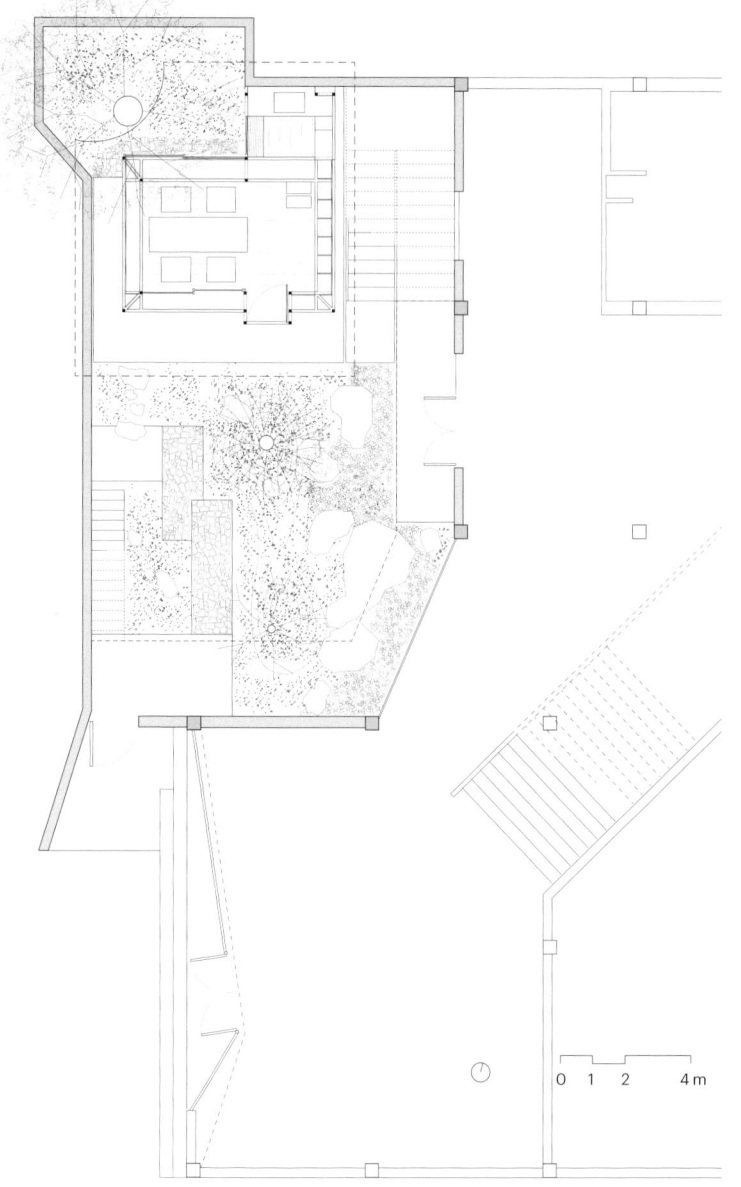

↗ Detail
↑ Exploded structural axonometric diagram
→ First-floor plan
↪ The paulownia leaning towards
  the tea house

0 1 2 4 m

Atelier Deshaus · Tea House in Li Garden · 200

Longteng Avenue, Xuhui, Shanghai, China

16

2015–2016

↗ The garden reflected in the glass

↪ Interior space
↳ Looking towards the tea house

Atelier Deshaus Tea House in Li Garden 202

Longteng Avenue, Xuhui, Shanghai, China

17 2015–2017
80,000-TON SILOS ART CENTER

3 Minsheng Road, Pudong District, Shanghai
Gross floor area: 16,322 m²

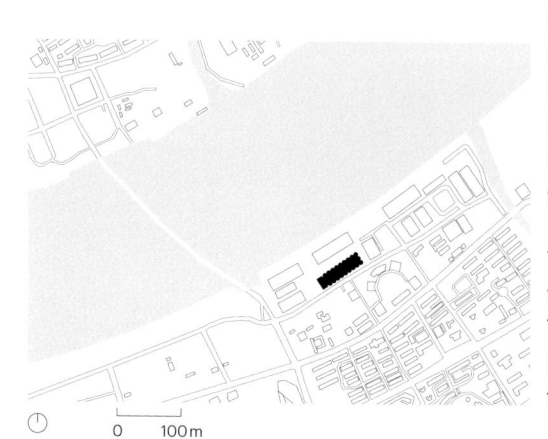

The 80,000-ton Silo, originally built in 1994, is one of the conserved industrial buildings located at the Minsheng Wharf in Shanghai's Pudong, its heritage value coming from its unique architecture type that is specific to its time. As an adaptive reuse of a historic building, planning studies and research by the architects were conducted to facilitate the development, where a new program of multi-functional art exhibition was eventually decided on, which would be suitable to both the neighborhood's development and the unique spatial characteristics of the existing building. Culture and art programs have become the main proponents in the public space productions of Shanghai's recent urban regeneration projects, in which art exhibition space is a good fit for the enclosed spaces of the existing silos.

The 2017 Shanghai Urban Space Art Season (SUSAS), which was a three-month exhibition, chose the silo for its main venue. The renovation of the silo was thus required to be completed rapidly within half a year, while also laying the groundwork for future renovations.

↖ Site plan
↦ View from across the river

3 Minsheng Road, Pudong District, Shanghai, China

17

2015–2017

↗ The bottom of the hanging escalator in collaboration with artist Zhan Wang
→ View from the east along the riverside

Atelier Deshaus   80,000-ton Silos Art Center   206

SUSAS mainly used the ground and top floors of the silos for its exhibitions. Because the silos are 48 meters tall, it is important to provide smooth circulation connecting, in addition to reorganizing the ground and top floor exhibition spaces, while also adding essential fire evacuation facilities. As silos, the functions of the former industrial structures necessitated spatial enclosure. In contrast, as a new public cultural infrastructure, it requires a spatial openness. The architecture strategy to dissolve the structure of the old form and the programmatic requirement of the new function is to hang, upon the north facade of the silos, an escalator that could directly connect the visitors from the second floor to the top floor. Not only does this strategy address the circulation needs, but the visitors also thus could enjoy the splendid view of the Huangpu River and the Minsheng Wharf. Except for this hanging escalator, the silos remain largely intact, preserving the original forms while the escalator showcases the new energy injected into old building.

The hanging escalator repositions the 80,000-ton Silos. By highlighting the river view to visitors, the proposal also announces its waterfront location, while bringing in the public spaces of the riverfront into the building. Thus, the architecture's public role is affirmed. The escalator also anticipates future renovations to the interior of the silos. In the proposal for future renovations, the thirty 12.5-meter-diameter silos will be cut and reconnected, and entered from different levels to form three-dimensional exhibition space.

In the future, the former grain carrier, which connected and transported grain from the riverside to the silo's second floor, will be transformed into an automatic pedestrian ramp. A continuous public space connecting the waterfront and the rooftop of the silos will be built.

↑ The wharf before the renovation

3 Minsheng Road, Pudong District, Shanghai, China

↗ View from the escalator towards Huangpu River
↪ Riverfront elevation
↳ The elevated channel connected to the building

3 Minsheng Road, Pudong District, Shanghai, China

↑ Lit-up escalator at dusk

3 Minsheng Road, Pudong District, Shanghai, China

17

↗ Model
→ Roof floor plan
↦ Seventh-floor plan
↦ Second-floor plan
↪ First-floor plan

Atelier Deshaus 80,000-ton Silos Art Center 212

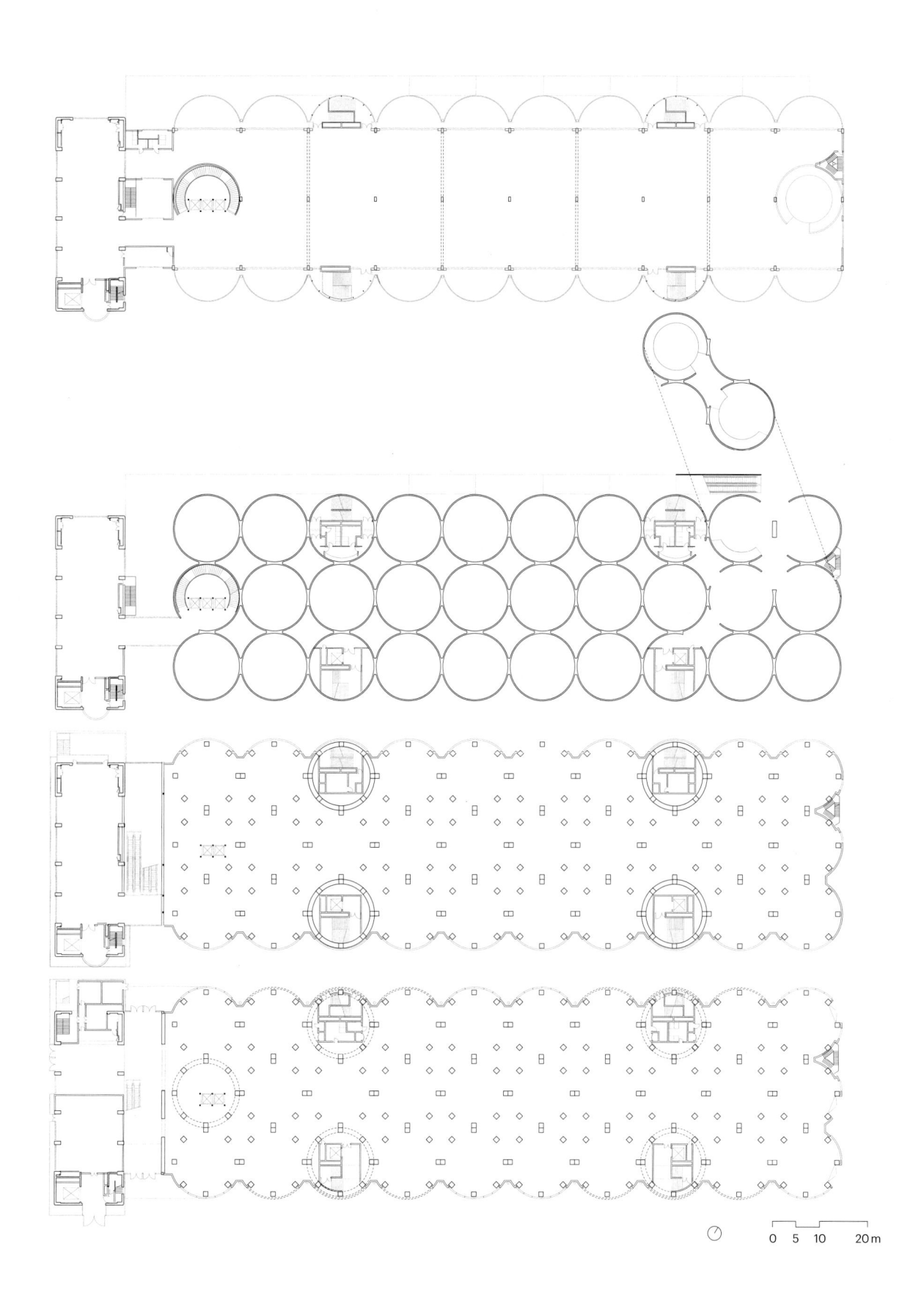

3 Minsheng Road, Pudong District, Shanghai, China

↗ Interior spiral stairs
→ View from inside towards Huangpu River
↘ Exhibition hall on the first floor

3 Minsheng Road, Pudong District, Shanghai, China

18   2016–2021
QINTAI ART MUSEUM

Wuhan City, Hubei Province
Floor area: 43,000 m²

Qintai Art Museum is located beside Moon Lake in Wuhan's Hanyang district, facing Meizi Hill across the lake to the south. In order to reduce the weight of the architectural mass on the natural surface of the lake, the shape of an undulating natural terrain has been used for the side facing the lake, while part of the exhibition area has been sunk beneath the ground. This both utilizes the underground space and minimizes the massing on the ground. This contrasts with the side facing the city road, where a vertical facade resolutely upholds the urbanity of the architecture.

The undulating roof is formed by an abstract stepped terrace that follows topographic contours. The risers of the steps are lined with a silver metallic surface, while the treads are covered with white stones or low vegetation. The roof is traversed by a number of winding stepped paths for pedestrians that are entirely open to the public, connecting Moon Lake with various parts of the museum—the exits from museum exhibition spaces, the designated space for public education, the art shop, and the café—and other public spaces. This allows them to create a public space framework that is independent of the museum's exhibition spaces. The activities of the public are part of the architectural surface.

The addition of an art museum has redefined urban space on the southern shore of Moon Lake. To the west of the museum the space is reserved for an urban plaza which will be the location of the planned Wuhan Library and Drama Centre. The main entrance to the museum, as well as those functions with strong public associations such as creative/cultural spaces, are all placed on this side, where a subtly inward-curving facade creates a sense of enclosure in conjunction with the location. From the plaza there are ramped paths linking to the second-floor café and rooftop terrace, establishing a public

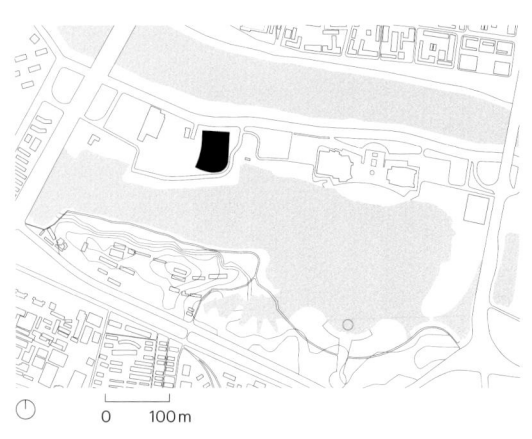

↖   Site plan
↪   Aerial view

circulation route that remains accessible after the museum closes. In operational terms, this strengthens the openness of the museum and the urbanity of the architecture.

The combination of the main hall and the undulating roofscape creates a unique venue for exhibitions. The exhibition space uses floating walls and eschews the notion of visitors taking a set route around a show. The walls function as surfaces for exhibiting art while also providing the structure that supports the undulating roof. The exhibition spaces for contemporary art, modern art, classical art, and special exhibitions display a high degree of functional flexibility, and can be independently accessed or sequentially linked.

Wuhan City, Hubei Province, China

↑ Terraced rooftop landscape
↑ The roof and the winding pathways
↪ Entrance to the pathways

Wuhan City, Hubei Province, China

↑ The museum with Moon Lake and Meizi Hill

Wuhan City, Hubei Province, China

18

2016–2021

Atelier Deshaus   Qintai Art Museum

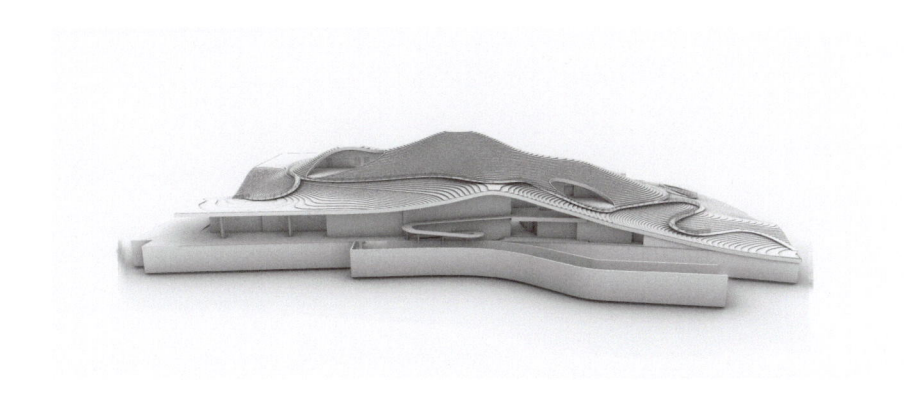

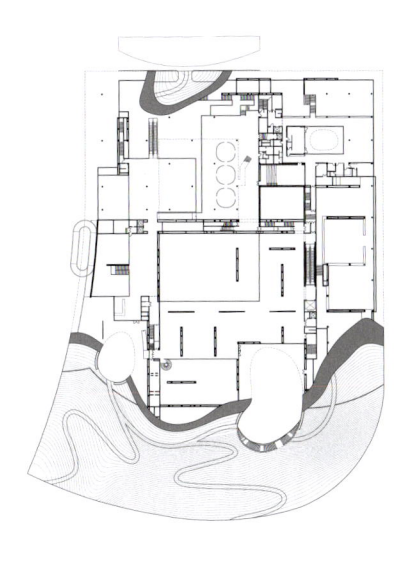

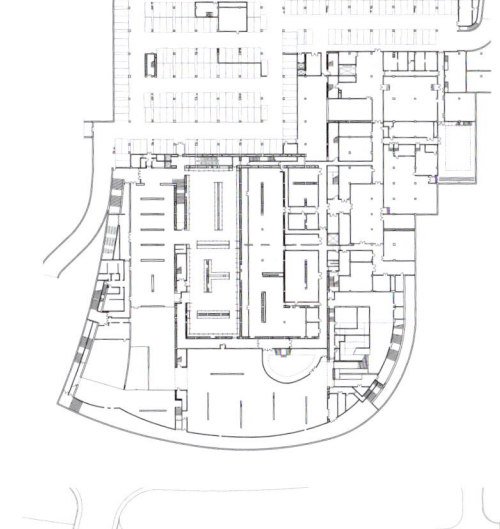

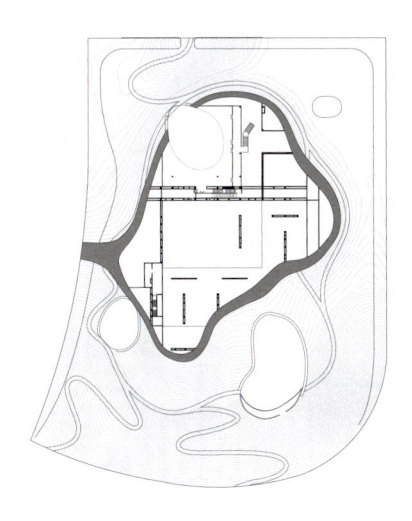

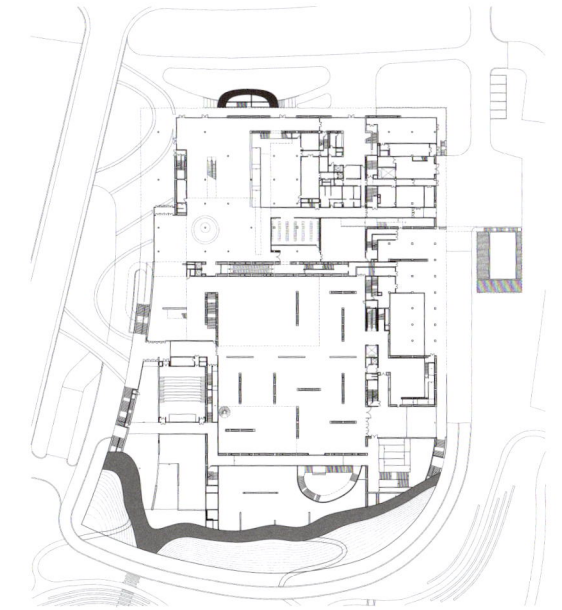

↖ Cultural/creative space and entrance hall
↑ Rendering
⌀ Plan (scale height 5.500–11.300), plan (scale height -6.600–0.000)
↓ Plan (scale height 11.300-top), plan (scale height 0.000–5.500)

0 25 50 m

Wuhan City, Hubei Province, China

223

18

2016–2021

↗ West elevation
→ Interior
↪ South & north elevation and section 1-1 & 2-2
↳ Detail

Atelier Deshaus   Qintai Art Museum   224

Wuhan City, Hubei Province, China

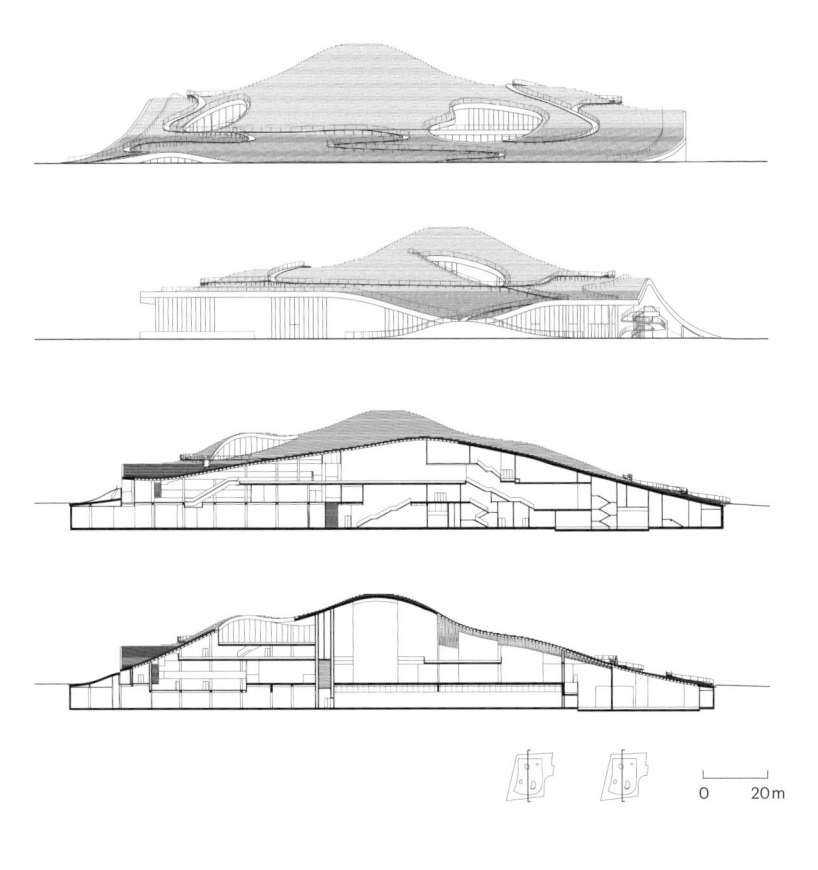

↗ Terraced rooftop landscape ↱ The north elevation
                                ↳ The roof and the winding pathways

Atelier Deshaus   Qintai Art Museum

Wuhan City, Hubei Province, China

↑　Contemporary exhibition hall on the first floor
↦　The entry hall of the underground exhibition hall

Wuhan City, Hubei Province, China

19   2017–2018

HOUSE ATO

South Square of National Stadium, Beijing
Floor area: 160 m²

Part of the exhibition *House Vision* held in Beijing in 2018, House ATO is an installation that rethinks the way humans live and the evolving spaces of dwelling.

In China before the 1980s, housing space was scarce and collective living was prominent. Kitchens lining up along a public corridor, shared bathrooms, and laundering spaces were all deformations to co-living spaces today. Compelled by such living conditions, nevertheless, there was a richness to the circumstance-inscribed neighborliness between families. For housing built after the 1980s, in order to prioritize the previously-deprived privacy, public spaces were limited, and housing design where one elevator opens onto two units per floor has resulted in neighbors that do not interact with each other. More recently, with the internet and social media, interpersonal interaction suddenly has again become an important part of the younger generation's daily lives. Human interaction is again being redefined.

For a long time, a dwelling has been an extension of the human body. Carefully observed, one could discover that the structural layers of human constructions have barely changed. From the primitive hut of Abbé Laugier to the four-millenia-old Chinese wooden architecture, to the modern dwelling such as Mies' Farnsworth House, the elements for constructing a house could be simplified into the three components or radicals that make up the Chinese character for dwelling, 舍 – 人 for rooftop, 中 for beam/support, and 口 for foundation/wall. Clearly, the history of construction by humanity precedes that even of the written word. The composition of "人中口" can be seen as a root metaphor, transcending different cultures.

The design of House ATO is a humble interpretation of these three elements. It uses structural elements from today's technology: 5-by-5-centimeter slender square columns and 5-centimeter thin roof. Even though technology can change material form, the fundamentals of spatial formation remain unchanged. Lifestyle shifts are manifested in the "face" of architecture. Ten interchangeable furniture boxes, as functional spaces for daily life, are inserted into the outermost layer, forming part of the building envelope and signifying a growing openness in contemporary life.

↦   View from afar

South Square of National Stadium, Beijing, China

↑ Night view

South Square of National Stadium, Beijing, China

19 House ATO is divided into three layers from the outside to the inside: an open and externalized space under the eaves, an openable/closable space formed by the flexible furniture units, and the most private oval bathroom. In the day, the space under the eaves and the furniture layer could be turned into a café, a ramen stall, a barber shop, or a meeting room. At night, the house returns to the intimate space of a home when all boxes are closed and living components are retrieved. The house is both a furnishing that could manifest the unique personality and lifestyle outlook of its dweller. It is also a neighborly space, just as the character 舍 denotes collectiveness: "to live in the city is called 舍 [市居曰舍]."

↗ Elevation
↪ Flexible furniture units
↪ Axonometric diagram
↪ Detail

Atelier Deshaus　　House ATO　　234

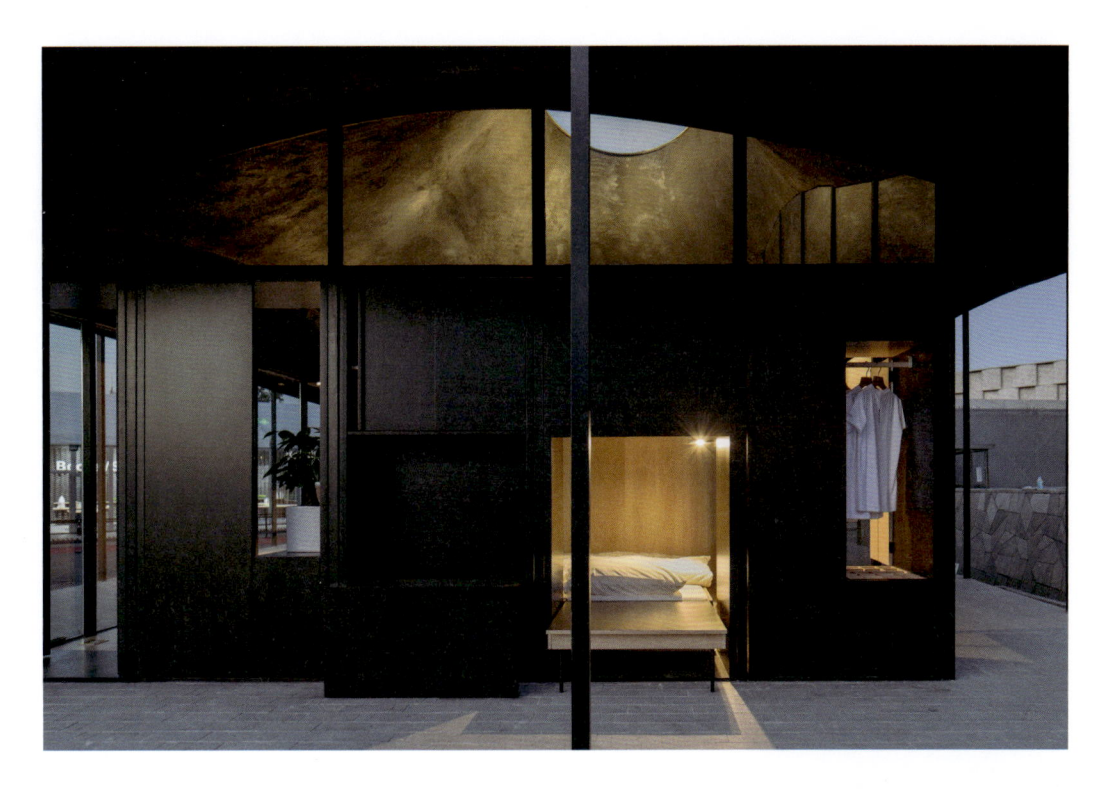

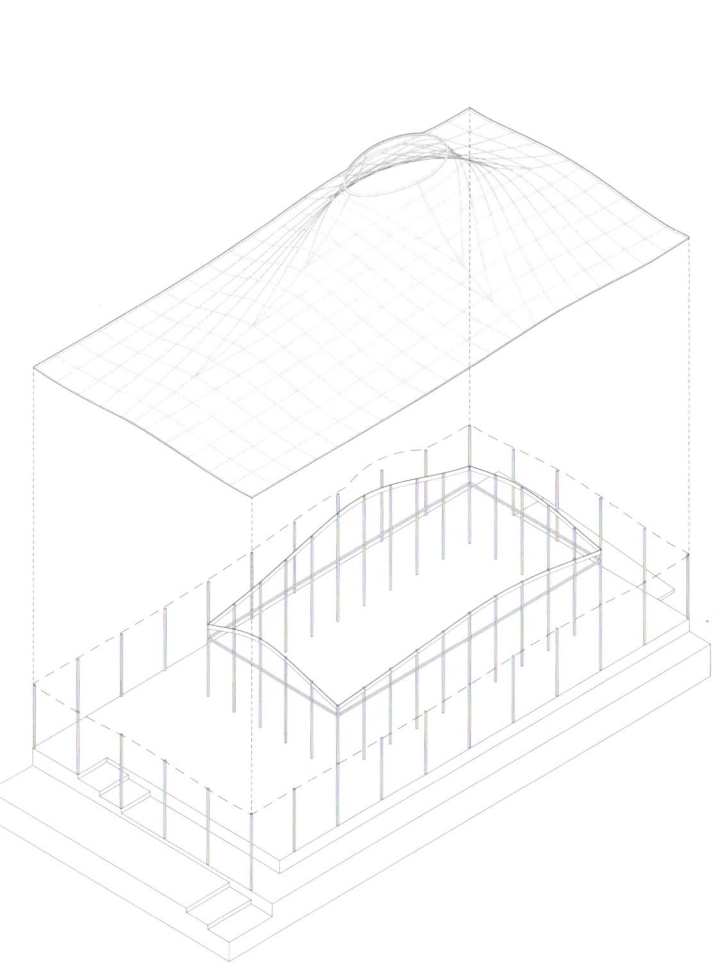

South Square of National Stadium, Beijing, China 235

19

2017–2018

Atelier Deshaus　　　House ATO　　　236

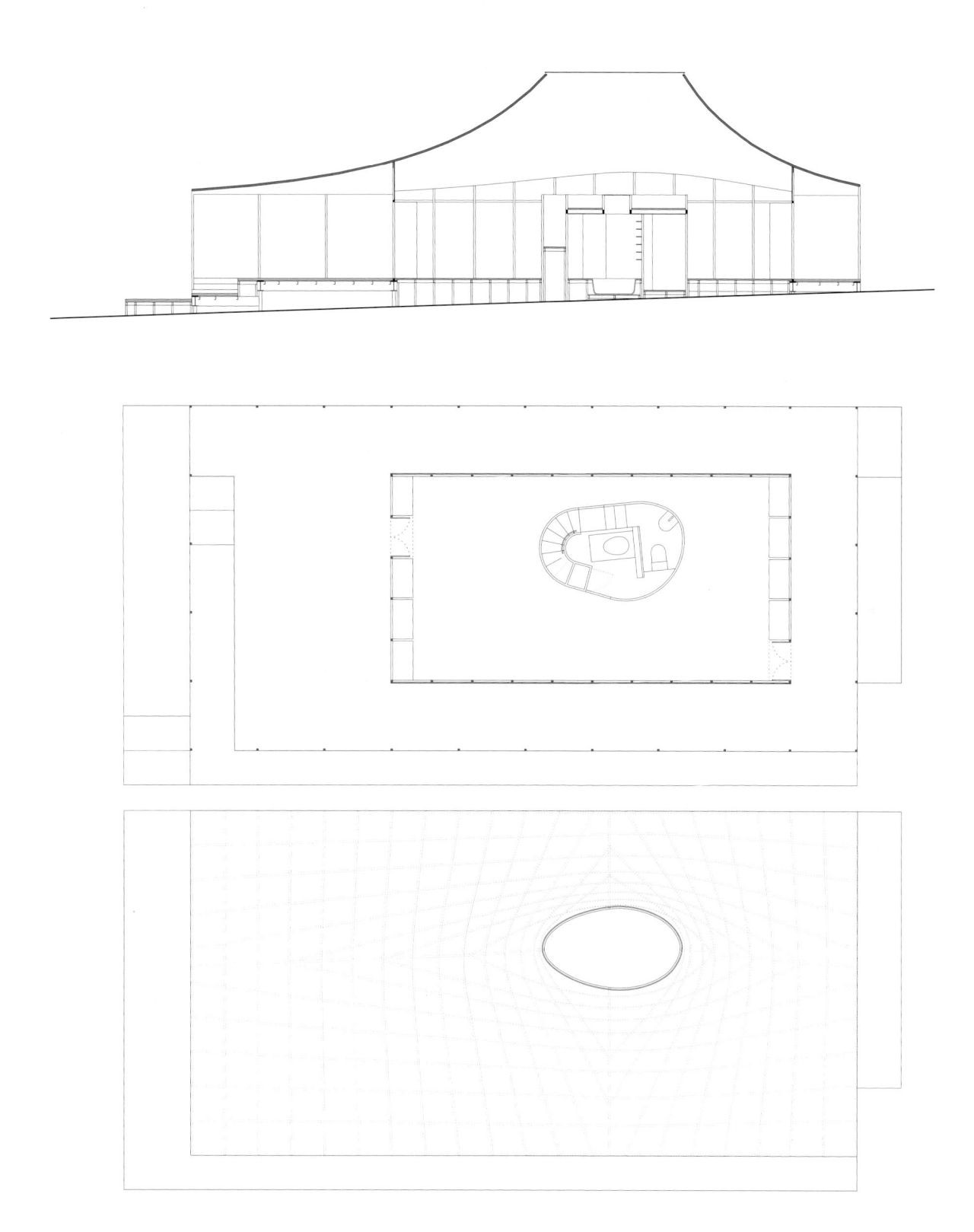

| Detail
↑ Section
∅ First-floor plan
↓ Roof plan

0 1 2   4m

South Square of National Stadium, Beijing, China

20 2018–2019
RIVERSIDE PASSAGE

2524 Yangshupu Road, Yangshupu Gas
Factory Wharf, Yangpu, Shanghai
Floor area: 268 m²

The site of Riverside Passage was once a wharf for unloading coal as part of the transportation system for the nearby Yangpu Gas Plant. The approximately 90-meter-long and 4-meter-high reinforced concrete wall along the wharf was built to prevent the unloaded coal from slipping into the river. Since losing its function for transporting coal, the long wall has endured an existence marked by silence and abandonment. Originally there were two walls, but the one along the river was dismantled long ago. Along the remaining wall, seeds have since landed in the gaps formed by the coal debris, broken concrete, and dust, where they have sprouted and grown into towering trees that complement the long wall. The trees and the abandoned wall together create a special, ruin-like ambience, one that is increasingly vanishing in Shanghai's recent urban renewal efforts that tend to be more and more delicate and polished. However, if a renewal project is to create a waterfront public space from somewhere previously used for industrial logistics, it is important to preserve the existing ambience because it bears witness to the sophisticated industries operating in Shanghai over the past half century.

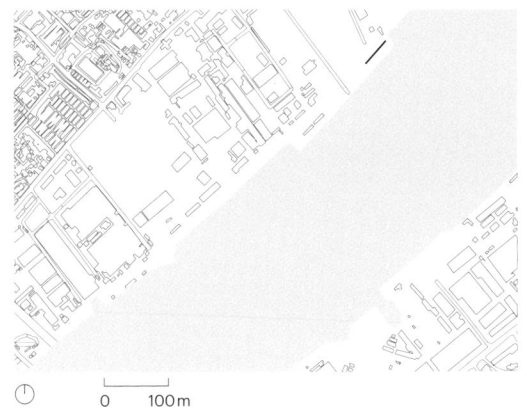

The new design takes the long solid concrete wall as a foundation for development—and one that has geological meaning. It serves as the basis not only for a sloping bridge connecting the flood-control wall and the gap of the wharf, traversing the wild vegetation, but also as the basis for an elevated open passage and a pavilion where people can take a rest. A single-pitched roof demarcates the inside and outside of the wall. On the inside, there is a passage at ground level facing a "garden" of ruins in the gap between the wharf and the shore. Facing outside there is a cantilevered corridor overlooking the river. Where one is grounded, the other is floating, suggesting the differences in our perception of distance and scale.

↖ Site plan
↱ The wharf after the renovation

Now it is no longer used for unloading coal, the wharf has been polished so it can function as a roller-skating rink; in conjunction with the cantilevered passage this establishes a spatial dialogue in closer proximity. The ground, the body of the wall, and the inserted structures create a new ensemble. Visitors may linger at will or continue moving through. The former coal wharf has thus become a place for urban flaneurs. The slender post-and-beam steel structures act as a series of frames for the urban views, so that when visitors move through, they begin to frame the assorted passing epochs: the chimney of the former gas plant, the bright-colored cranes, tide-washed concrete blocks embedded in mud, buildings rising across the river, and the bridges in the distance.

Yangshupu Gas Factory Wharf, Yangpu, Shanghai, China

20

2018–2019

Atelier Deshaus   Riverside Passage

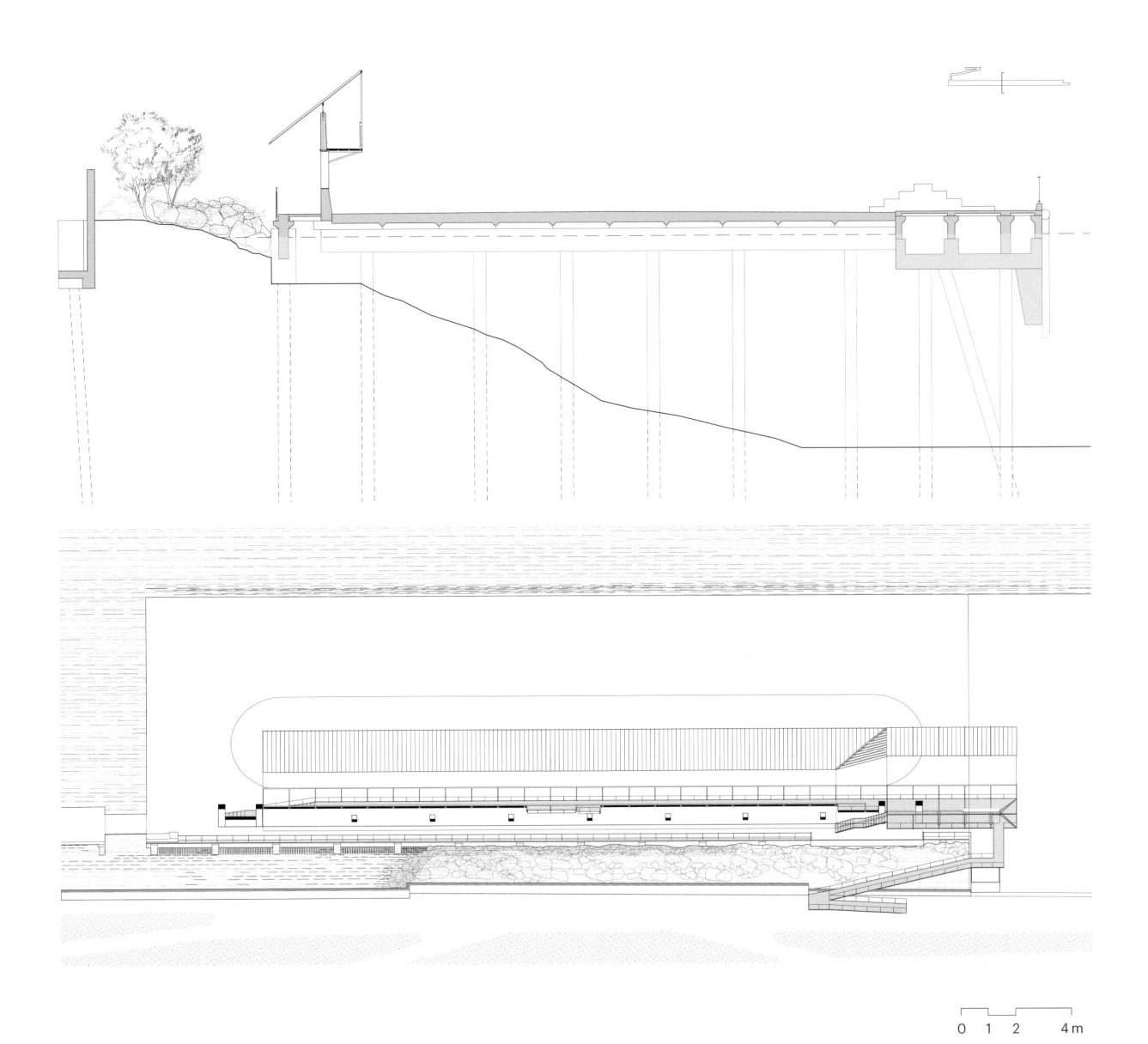

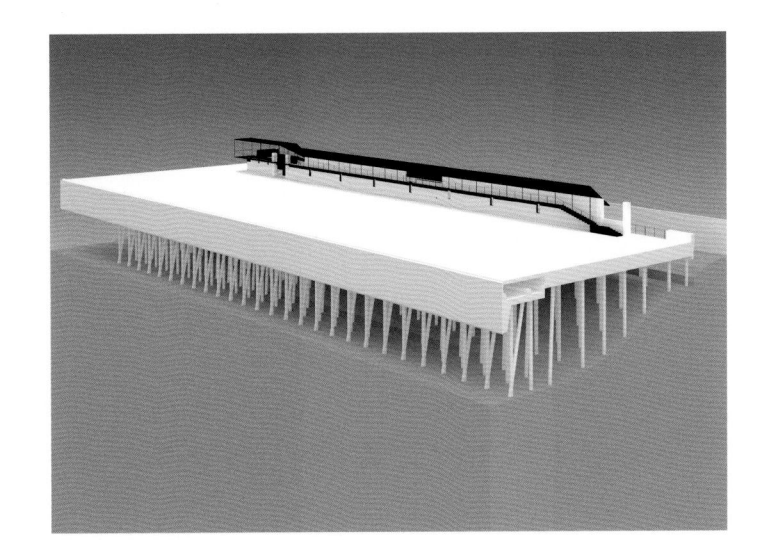

← Detail
↑ Section
∅ Axonometric diagram
→ Rendering

Yangshupu Gas Factory Wharf, Yangpu, Shanghai, China

241

↑ The lit-up wharf at dusk

Yangshupu Gas Factory Wharf, Yangpu, Shanghai, China

20

2018–2019

↑   North end

Atelier Deshaus   Riverside Passage   244

↑ Detail

Yangshupu Gas Factory Wharf, Yangpu, Shanghai, China

20

↗ The new structure upon the old wall
↓ Aerial view from above the roof

↑ The garden on the inside of the wall
↓ The elevated walkway with river view

Yangshupu Gas Factory Wharf, Yangpu, Shanghai, China

↕ The garden of ruins

↑   The wall, the window opening, and the roof creating new architectural integrity
↓   The passage and the garden

↑ The ramp crossing the gap between the wharf and the flood control wall

Yangshupu Gas Factory Wharf, Yangpu, Shanghai, China

INDEX

Page 36 01 2003–2005
XIAYU KINDERGARTEN
Location: 301 Huale Road, Qingpu District, Shanghai
Design Team: Chen Yifeng, Liu Yichun, Zhuang Shen, Fan Minji
Collaboration: Tongji Architectural Design (Group) Co., Ltd.
Client: Shanghai Qingpu Housing Development Administration
Floor Area: 6,328 m^2
Design Period: 2003.08–2004.04
Completion: 2005.01

44 02 2006–2008
R&D CENTER IN JISHAN SOFTWARE PARK IN NANJING
Location: Nanjing, Jiangsu Province
Design Team: Chen Yifeng, Liu Yichun, Zhuang Shen, Chen Juan
Collaboration: Tongji Architectural Design (Group) Co., Ltd.
Client: Jiangsu Software Park Development & Construction Co., Ltd.
Floor Area: 12,000 m^2
Design Period: 2006.05–2006.12
Completion: 2008.07

52 03 2008–2010
KINDERGARTEN IN JIADING NEW TOWN
Location: 933 Hongde Road, Jiading District, Shanghai
Design Team: Chen Yifeng, Liu Yichun,
Zhuang Shen, Wang Shuyi, Liu Qian
Collaboration: Tongji Architectural Design (Group) Co., Ltd
Client: Shanghai Jiading Education Bureau
Floor Area: 6,600 m^2
Design Period: 2008.04–2008.12
Completion: 2010.03

62 04 2009–2012
QINGPU YOUTH CENTER
Location: 268 Huake Road, Qingpu District, Shanghai
Design Team: Liu Yichun, Chen Yifeng, Gao Lin, Liu Qian, Wang Longhai
Collaboration: Tongji Architectural Design (Group) Co., Ltd
Client: Shanghai Qingpu State-Owned Assets
Supervision and Administration Commission
Floor Area: 6,612 m^2
Design Period: 2009.07–2010.01
Completion: 2012.02

Atelier Deshaus · Catalog of Featured Works

72   05   2009-2011
              SPIRAL GALLERY I
              Location: Ziqidonglai Park, Tianzhu Road, Jiading District, Shanghai
              Design Team: Liu Yichun, Chen Yifeng, Fan Beilei
              Collaboration: Shanghai Building Materials Industrial
              Design and Research Institute Co., Ltd.
              Client: Shanghai Jiading New Town Development Co., Ltd
              Floor Area: 250 m^2
              Design Period: 2009.09-2010.02
              Completion: 2011.06

80   06   2010-2015
              R&D CENTER OF SHANGHAI INTERNATIONAL
              AUTOMOBILE CITY IN JIADING
              Location: Anhong Road, Jiading District, Shanghai
              Design Team: Chen Yifeng, Liu Yichun, Song Chongfang,
              Wang Longhai, Fan Beilei
              Collaboration: Shanghai Institute of Shanghai
              Architectural Design & Research Co., Ltd.
              Client: Shanghai International Automobile City Development Co., Ltd.
              Floor Area: 36,600 m^2
              Design Period: 2010.01-2012.12
              Completion: 2015.06

90   07   2010-2015
              TAO LI YUAN SCHOOL IN JIADING
              Location: 2065 Shuping Road, Jiading District, Shanghai
              Design Team: Liu Yichun, Chen Yifeng, Gao Lin, Wang Longhai, Fan Beilei,
              Song Chongfang, Wu Zhenghui
              Collaboration: Shanghai Jiangnan Architectural
              Design Institute (Group) Co., Ltd.
              Client: State-owned Assets Supervision and
              Administration Commission of Jiading District
              Floor Area: 35,688 m^2
              Design Period: 2010.05-2012.12
              Completion: 2015.03

98   08   2011-2014
              LONG MUSEUM WEST BUND
              Location: 3398 Longteng Avenue, Xuhui District, Shanghai
              Design Team: Liu Yichun, Chen Yifeng, Wang Longhai, Wang Weishi,
              Wu Zhenghui, Wang Xuipei, Chen Kun
              Collaboration: Tongji Architectural Design (Group) Co., Ltd
              Client: Shanghai Xuhui Binjiang Development
              Investment Construction Co.,Ltd.
              Floor Area: 33,007 m^2
              Design Period: 2011.10-2012.07
              Completion: 2014.03

114　　09　　2013–2015
　　　　　　 HUAXIN CONFERENCE HUB
　　　　　　 Location: 142 Tianlin Road, Xuhui District, Shanghai
　　　　　　 Design Team: Chen Yifeng, Liu Yichun, Gao Lin, Wu Zhenghui, Ma Danhong
　　　　　　 Collaboration: Shanghai Architectural Design Research Institute Co., Ltd.
　　　　　　 Client: SVA Real Estate Co.,Ltd.
　　　　　　 Floor Area: 1,000 m²
　　　　　　 Design Period: 2013.07–2015.08
　　　　　　 Completion: 2015.12

122　　10　　2014–2017
　　　　　　 ONE FOUNDATION KINDERGARTEN IN XINCHANG COUNTY
　　　　　　 Location: Xinchang County, Tianquan, Sichuan Province
　　　　　　 Design Team: Chen Yifeng, Liu Yichun, Gao Lin, Gao De
　　　　　　 Collaboration: Beijing Tongcheng Fanhua Construction
　　　　　　 Engineering Consulting Co.,Ltd.
　　　　　　 Client: One Foundation
　　　　　　 Floor Area: 1,500 m²
　　　　　　 Design Period: 2014.10–2015.04
　　　　　　 Completion: 2017.01

134　　11　　2014–2015
　　　　　　 ATELIER DESHAUS OFFICE ON WEST BUND
　　　　　　 Location: 2555-16 Longteng Avenue, Xuhui District, Shanghai
　　　　　　 Design Team: Liu Yichun, Chen Yifeng, Wang Longhai, Wang Weishi
　　　　　　 Collaboration: Tongji Architectural Design (Group) Co., Ltd
　　　　　　 Client: Atelier Deshaus
　　　　　　 Floor Area: 430 m²
　　　　　　 Design Period: 2014.11–2015.04
　　　　　　 Completion: 2015.11

144　　12　　2015–2019
　　　　　　 YUNYANG RIVERFRONT VISITOR CENTER
　　　　　　 Location: Binjiang Avenue, Yunyang County, Chongqing
　　　　　　 Design Team: Chen Yifeng, Gao Lin, Song Chongfang, Wang Xuepei
　　　　　　 Collaboration: CMCU Engineering Co., Ltd.
　　　　　　 Client: Immigration Bureau of Yunyang County, Yunyang Urban Development & Investment (Group) Co., Ltd.
　　　　　　 Floor Area: 9,011 m²
　　　　　　 Design Period: 2015.01–2016.08
　　　　　　 Completion: 2019.10

154	13	2015 BLOSSOM PAVILION Location: 570 West Huaihai Road, Shanghai Design Team: Liu Yichun, Wang Longhai, Ding Jieru Collaboration: AND Office, Zhan Wang Client: Shanghai Urban Sculpture Art Center Floor Area: 96 m^2 Design Period: 2015.04–2015.10 Completion: 2015.11
162	14	2015–2019 TAIZHOU CONTEMPORARY ART MUSEUM Location: Fengshan Road, Taizhou, Zhejiang Province Design Team: Liu Yichun, Chen Yifeng, Shen Wen Collaboration: AND Office Client: Taizhou Shimao Culture & Innovation Development Co. Ltd. Floor Area: 2,454 m^2 Design Period: 2015.05–2015.09 Completion: 2019.04
176	15	2015–2016 MODERN ART MUSEUM SHANGHAI AND ITS WALKWAYS Location: 4777 Binjiang Avenue, Pudong District, Shanghai Design Team: Liu Yichun, Chen Yifeng, Wang Weishi, Shen Wen, Chen Hao, Wang Longhai, Chan Hiongai, Ding Jieru, Zhou Mengdie Collaboration: Tongji Architectural Design (Group) Co., Ltd, AND Office Client: Shanghai East Bund Investment (Group) Co., Ltd. Floor Area: 9,180 m^2 Design Period: 2015.05–2016.10 Completion: 2016.12
194	16	2015–2016 TEA HOUSE IN LI GARDEN Location: 2555 Longteng Avenue, Xuhui District, Shanghai Design Team: Liu Yichun, Shen Wen, Wang Weishi Collaboration: AND Office Client: Guangdong Fang Suo Culture Investment Development Co.,Ltd. Floor Area: 19 m^2 Design Period: 2015.09–2015.12 Completion: 2016.06

204	17	2015–2017

80,000-TON SILOS ART CENTER ON MINSHENG WHARF
Location: 3 Minsheng Road, Pudong District, Shanghai
Design Team: Liu Yichun, Chen Yifeng, Chan Hiongai,
Wang Longhai, Wang Weishi
Collaboration: Tongji Architectural Design (Group) Co., Ltd, AND Office
Client: Shanghai East Bund Investment (Group) Co., Ltd.
Floor Area: 16,322 m^2
Design Period: 2015.10–2017.10
Completion: 2017.10

216	18	2016–2021

QINTAI ART MUSEUM
Location: Zhiyin Avenue, Hanyang District, Wuhan, Hubei Province
Design Team: Liu Yichun, Chen Yu, Wang Longhai, Hu Chenchen, Chen Hao, Shen Wen, Chen Chihhan, Tang Yun, Zhang Xiaoqi, Wu Wenchao, Deng Rui, Liu Xin, Pang Zirui, Wang Jiawen, Cao Ye
Collaboration: Wuhan Architectural Design Institute
Client: Wuhan City Construction Group Co., Ltd.
Floor Area: 43,000 m^2
Design Period: 2016.05–2018.09
Completion: 2021.12

230	19	2017–2018

HOUSE ATO
Location: South Piazza of the National Stadium
Design Team: Liu Yichun, Shen Wen, Deng Rui, Gong Yu
Collaboration: AND Office
Client: China House Vision Curation Committee
Floor Area: 160 m^2
Design Period: 2017.01–2018.04
Completion: 2018.09

238	20	2018–2019

RIVERSIDE PASSAGE
Location: 2524 Yangshupu Rd, Yangshupu Gas Factory Wharf, Yangpu, Shanghai
Planning: Atelier Z+, Atelier Liu Yuyang Architects, Atelier Deshaus
Structural Design: AND Office
Design Team: Liu Yichun, Shen Wen, Chan Hiongai
Coordination: Zhang Bin, Wang Weijie, Wang Jiaqi, Guo Yifeng
Landscape Consultant: YIYU Design, Laurent Landscape&Architects Firm
Floor Area: 268 m^2
Design Period: 2018.03–2018.11
Completion: 2019.10

PROJECTS REALISED BY ATELIER DESHAUS

01 TRI-HOUSE
   Location: Kunshan, Jiangsu Province
   Design Team: Zhuang Shen, Liu Yichun, Chen Yifeng
   Collaboration: Kunshan Architectural Design Institute
   Client: Kunshan Xinyan Real Estate Development Co., Ltd.
   Floor Area: 460 m^2
   Design Period: 2001.05–2001.07
   Completion: 2002.03

02 COLLEGE OF LITERATURE AND MEDIA OF
   DONGGUAN UNIVERSITY OF TECHNOLOGY
   Location: Dongguan, Guangdong Province
   Design Team: Chen Yifeng, Liu Yichun, Zhuang Shen
   Collaboration: Tongji Architectural Design (Group) Co., Ltd.
   Client: Office of New Campus Construction of
   Dongguan University of Technology
   Floor Area: 9,150 m^2
   Design Period: 2002.07–2003.01
   Completion: 2004.05

03 SCHOOL OF ELECTRICAL ENGINEERING & INTELLIGENTIZATION
   OF DONGGUAN UNIVERSITY OF TECHNOLOGY
   Location: Dongguan, Guangdong Province
   Design Team: Liu Yichun, Zhuang Shen, Chen Yifeng
   Collaboration: Tongji Architectural Design (Group) Co., Ltd.
   Client: Office of New Campus Construction of
   Dongguan University of Technology
   Floor Area: 20,860 m^2
   Design Period: 2002.07–2003.01
   Completion: 2004.08

04 COLLEGE OF COMPUTER OF DONGGUAN UNIVERSITY OF TECHNOLOGY
   Location: Dongguan, Guangdong Province
   Design Team: Zhuang Shen, Liu Yichun, Chen Yifeng
   Collaboration: Tongji Architectural Design (Group) Co., Ltd.
   Client: Office of New Campus Construction of
   Dongguan University of Technology
   Floor Area: 15,310 m^2
   Design Period: 2002.07–2003.01
   Completion: 2004.05

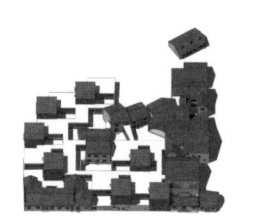

05 XIAYU KINDERGARTEN
    Location: 301 Huale Road, Qingpu District, Shanghai
    Design Team: Chen Yifeng, Liu Yichun, Zhuang Shen, Fan Minji
    Collaboration: Tongji Architectural Design (Group) Co., Ltd.
    Client: Shanghai Qingpu Housing Development Administration
    Floor Area: 6,328 m^2
    Design Period: 2003.08-2004.04
    Completion: 2005.01

06 OFFICE BUILDING FOR QINGPU BUSINESS ASSOCIATION
    Location: Qinglong Road, Qingpu District, Shanghai
    Design Team: Zhuang Shen, Chen Yifeng, Liu Yichun, Tang Yu
    Collaboration: Shanghai Weilian Structural Design Co., Ltd., Shanghai Yemao Construction Co., Ltd.
    Client: Shanghai Administration of Industry and Commerce (Qingpu Branch)
    Floor Area: 6,745 m^2
    Design Period: 2003.12-2004.06
    Completion: 2005.07

07 PORT INSPECTOR STATION OF ZHUJIAJIAO, QINGPU
    Location: Jiulong Road, Qingpu District, Shanghai
    Design Team: Chen Yifeng, Liu Yichun, Zhuang Shen, Zhang Yi
    Collaboration: Shanghai Weilian Structural Design Co., Ltd., Shanghai Yemao Construction Co., Ltd.
    Client: Shanghai Zhujiajiao Investment and Development Co., Ltd
    Floor Area: 360 m^2
    Design Period: 2004.10-2005.06
    Completion: 2006.12

08 TIANTIAN KINDERGARTEN OF QINGPU
    Location: Wushebang Road, Qingpu District, Shanghai
    Design Team: Liu Yichun, Chen Yifeng, Zhuang Shen, Peng Xu
    Client: Shanghai Qingpu New Town Development (Group) Co., Ltd.
    Floor Area: 4,500 m^2
    Design Period: 2005.07-2006.01

Atelier Deshaus   Catalog of Works

09 ZHU'S CLUBHOUSE
   Location: Zhujiajiao Town, Qingpu District, Shanghai
   Design Team: Zhuang Shen, Liu Yichun, Chen Yifeng, He Yong
   Collaboration: Tongji Architectural Design (Group) Co., Ltd.
   Client: Hongda Construction (Group) Co., Ltd.
   Floor Area: 1,000 m^2
   Design Period: 2006.03–2006.09

10 R&D CENTER IN JISHAN SOFTWARE PARK
   Location: Nanjing, Jiangsu Province
   Design Team: Chen Yifeng, Liu Yichun, Zhuang Shen, Chen Juan
   Collaboration: Tongji Architectural Design (Group) Co., Ltd.
   Client: Jiangsu Software Park Development & Construction Co., Ltd.
   Floor Area: 12,000 m^2
   Design Period: 2006.05–2006.12
   Completion: 2008.07

11 PLOT 7 OF JISHAN SOFTWARE PARK
   Location: Nanjing, Jiangsu Province
   Design Team: Chen Yifeng, Liu Yichun, Zhuang Shen, Chen Juan
   Collaboration: Tongji Architectural Design (Group) Co., Ltd.
   Floor Area: 8,000 m^2
   Design Period: 2006.05–2006.12
   Completion: 2008.07

12 TEA HOUSE OF JISHAN SOFTWARE PARK
   Location: Nanjing, Jiangsu Province
   Design Team: Chen Yifeng, Liu Yichun, Zhuang Shen, Chen Juan
   Collaboration: Tongji Architectural Design (Group) Co., Ltd.
   Client: Jiangsu Software Park Development & Construction Co., Ltd.
   Floor Area: 571 m^2
   Design Period: 2006.05–2006.12
   Completion: 2008.07

13 QINGPU HYDROLOGICAL SURVEY STATION
   Location: Haiying Road, Qingpu District, Shanghai
   Design Team: Liu Yichun, Chen Yifeng, Zhuang Shen, Peng Xu, Liu Qian, Wang Longhai
   Collaboration: Shanghai Yaxin Construction Consulting Co., Ltd.
   Client: Qingpu Hydrology Team
   Floor Area: 1,840 m^2
   Design Period: 2006.12–2011.06

14 E HOTEL OF ART VILLAGE IN XIXI WETLAND
   Location: Hangzhou, Zhejiang Province
   Design Team: Liu Yichun, Chen Yifeng, Zhuang Shen, Wang Longhai, Wang Yue
   Collaboration: Shanghai Yaxin Construction Consultant Co., Ltd.
   Client: Construction Headquarters of Xixi Wetland National Park (Phase III)
   Floor Area: 6,400 m²
   Design Period: 2008.01-2009.01

15 PLANNING EXHIBITION CENTER OF JIADING NEW TOWN
   Location: Yining Road, Jiading District, Shanghai
   Design Team: Zhuang Shen, Liu Yichun, Chen Yifeng, Huang Dong, Zhou Jing
   Collaboration: Tongji Architectural Design (Group) Co., Ltd
   Client: Shanghai Jiading New Town Development Co., Ltd
   Floor Area: 2,250 m²
   Design Period: 2008.01-2009.02
   Completion: 2009.09

16 ADMINISTRATION BUILDING OF GAS COMPANY OF JIADING NEW TOWN
   Location: Yining Road, Jiading District, Shanghai
   Design Team: Chen Yifeng, Liu Yichun, Zhuang Shen, Liu Qian
   Collaboration: Tongji Architectural Design (Group) Co., Ltd
   Client: Shanghai Jiading New Town Development Co., Ltd
   Floor Area: 2,250 m²
   Design Period: 2008.03-2008.09
   Completion: 2009.09

17 KINDERGARTEN IN JIADING NEW TOWN
   Location: 933 Hongde Road, Jiading District, Shanghai
   Design Team: Chen Yifeng, Liu Yichun,
   Zhuang Shen, Wang Shuyi, Liu Qian
   Collaboration: Tongji Architectural Design (Group) Co., Ltd
   Client: Shanghai Jiading Education Bureau
   Floor Area: 6,600 m²
   Design Period: 2008.04-2008.12
   Completion: 2010.03

18 YUE'S HOUSE AND STUDIO
   Location: Dayu Village, Jiading District, Shanghai
   Design Team: Liu Yichun, Chen Yifeng, Wang Longhai
   Collaboration: Shanghai Yaxin Construction Consultant Co., Ltd.
   Client: Private
   Floor Area: 1,400 m²
   Design Period: 2008.07-2009.09

19 PUBLIC RESTROOM IN DIANSHANHU GREENLAND IN QINGPU
   Location: Dianshanhu Avenue, Qingpu District, Shanghai
   Design Team: Liu Yichun, Chen Yifeng, Wang Longhai
   Collaboration: Shanghai Yaxin Construction Consultant Co., Ltd.
   Client: Shanghai Qingpu New Town Development Co., Ltd
   Floor Area: 107 m^2
   Design Period: 2009.03–2009.06
   Completion: 2010.11

20 NINGGUO ZEN TEMPLE
   Location: Huajing Road, Xuhui District, Shanghai
   Design Team: Liu Yichun, Chen Yifeng, Wang Longhai
   Client: Ningguo Zen Temple
   Floor Area: 7,000 m^2
   Design Period: 2009.05–2009.10

21 QINGPU YOUTH CENTER
   Location: 268 Huake Road, Qingpu District, Shanghai
   Design Team: Liu Yichun, Chen Yifeng, Gao Lin, Liu Qian, Wang Longhai
   Collaboration: Tongji Architectural Design (Group) Co., Ltd
   Client: Shanghai Qingpu State-Owned Assets
   Supervision and Administration Commission
   Floor Area: 6,612 m^2
   Design Period: 2009.07–2010.01
   Completion: 2012.02

22 SPIRAL GALLERY I
   Location: Ziqidonglai Park, Tianzhu Road, Jiading District, Shanghai
   Design Team: Liu Yichun, Chen Yifeng, Fan Beilei
   Collaboration: Shanghai Building Materials Industrial
   Design and Research Institute Co., Ltd.
   Client: Shanghai Jiading New Town Development Co., Ltd
   Floor Area: 250 m^2
   Design Period: 2009.09–2010.02
   Completion: 2011.06

23 SPIRAL GALLERY II
   Location: Ziqidonglai Park, Tianzhu Road, Jiading District, Shanghai
   Design Team: Chen Yifeng, Liu Yichun, Li Jun
   Collaboration: Shanghai Building Materials Industrial
   Design and Research Institute Co., Ltd.
   Client: Shanghai Jiading New Town Development Co., Ltd
   Floor Area: 500 m^2
   Design Period: 2009.09–2010.02
   Completion: 2011.06

24 R&D CENTER OF SHANGHAI INTERNATIONAL
AUTOMOBILE CITY IN JIADING
Location: Anhong Road, Jiading District, Shanghai
Design Team: Chen Yifeng, Liu Yichun, Song Chongfang,
Wang Longhai, Fan Beilei
Collaboration: Shanghai Institute of Shanghai
Architectural Design & Research Co., Ltd.
Client: Shanghai International Automobile City Development Co., Ltd.
Floor Area: 36,600 m²
Design Period: 2010.01–2012.12
Completion: 2015.06

25 ORDOS 2010 P9 OFFICE BUILDING
Location: Dongsheng District, Ordos, Inner Mongolia Province
Design Team: Liu Yichun, Chen Yifeng, Wang Longhai
Client: Shengbang Investment Co., Ltd
Floor Area: 13,500 m²
Design Period: 2010.02–2010.09

26 ORDOS 2010 T7 OFFICE BUILDING
Location: Dongsheng District, Ordos, Inner Mongolia Province
Design Team: Liu Yichun, Chen Yifeng, Gao Lin
Client: Shengbang Investment Co., Ltd
Floor Area: 15,100 m²
Design Period: 2010.02–2010.09

27 DAYU ARTIST VILLAGE
Location: Dayu Village, Jiading District, Shanghai
Design Team: Liu Yichun, Chen Yifeng, Wang Shuyi, Li Jun, Wang Longhai
Collaboration: Tongji Architectural Design (Group) Co., Ltd
Client: Urban Construction Office of Malu Town, Jiading, Shanghai
Floor Area: 6,500 m²
Design Period: 2010.02–2010.09

28 TAO LI YUAN SCHOOL IN JIADING
Location: 2065 Shuping Road, Jiading District, Shanghai
Design Team: Liu Yichun, Chen Yifeng, Gao Lin, Wang Longhai, Fan Beilei, Song Chongfang, Wu Zhenghui
Collaboration: Shanghai Jiangnan Architectural
Design Institute (Group) Co., Ltd.
Client: State-owned Assets Supervision and
Administration Commission of Jiading District
Floor Area: 35,688 m²
Design Period: 2010.05–2012.12
Completion: 2015.03

29 DING YI BUILDING OF ARTRON (SHANGHAI) ART CENTER
    Location: 1022 Jialuo Road, Jiading District, Shanghai
    Design Team: Liu Yichun, Chen Yifeng, Wang Longhai, Fan Beilei, Chen Kun
    Collaboration: Shanghai Dujuan Design and Consulting Co., Ltd.
    Client: Shanghai Artron Printing Co., Ltd.
    Floor Area: 750 m^2
    Design Period: 2010.11–2013.11
    Completion: 2014.05

30 LONG MUSEUM WEST BUND
    Location: 3398 Longteng Avenue, Xuhui District, Shanghai
    Design Team: Liu Yichun, Chen Yifeng, Wang Longhai, Wang Weishi, Wu Zhenghui, Wang Xuipei, Chen Kun
    Collaboration: Tongji Architectural Design (Group) Co., Ltd
    Client: Shanghai Xuhui Binjiang Development Investment Construction Co.,Ltd.
    Floor Area: 33,007 m^2
    Design Period: 2011.10–2012.07
    Completion: 2014.03

31 LINGYUN COMMUNITY SERVICE CENTER
    Location: Lingyun Road, Xuhui District, Shanghai
    Design Team: Chen Yifeng, Liu Yichun, Li Jun, Song Chongfang, Zuo Long, Gao De
    Collaboration: Tongji Architectural Design (Group) Co., Ltd
    Client: Lingyun Road Sub-district Office, Xuhui District, Shanghai
    Floor Area: 16,860 m^2
    Design Period: 2011.12–2015.05
    Completion: 2017.10

32 SHANGHAI XUHUI HIGH SCHOOL (HUAFA ROAD CAMPUS)
    Location: 68 Huafa Road, Xuhui District, Shanghai
    Design Team: Liu Yichun, Chen Yifeng, Wang Weishi, Wu Zhenghui, Song Chongfang, Zuo Long
    Collaboration: Tongji Architectural Design (Group) Co., Ltd
    Client: Shanghai Xuhui Education Bureau, Shanghai Xuhui Housing Administration Bureau
    Floor Area: 20,280 m^2
    Design Period: 2012.05–2015.04
    Completion: 2018.05

33 RENOVATION OF LONGHUA TEMPLE
   (FIRST PLACE IN THE COMPETITION)
   Location: Longhua Road, Xuhui District, Shanghai
   Design Team: Liu Yichun, Chen Yifeng, Gao Lin, Wang Weishi, Wu Zhenghui
   Client: Shanghai Longhua Construction & Development Co., Ltd.
   Floor Area: Plot A: 10,750 m², Plot D: 24,800 m²
   Design Period: 2012.06–2012.08

34 FOOTBRIDGE ON RIHUI RIVER
   Location: Intersection of Rihui River and Huangpu River, Shanghai
   Design Team: Liu Yichun, Wang Weishi
   Collaboration: Zhang Zhun, Shanghai Urban
   Construction & Design Research Institute Co., Ltd.
   Client: Shanghai Shenjiang Liang'an Development
   Construction Investment(Group)Co.,Ltd.
   Design Period: 2012.10–2015.12
   Completion: 2016.09

35 RIVERSIDE RESTAURANT ON WEST BUND
   Location: Longteng Avenue, Xuhui District, Shanghai
   Design Team: Liu Yichun, Chen Yifeng, Wang Longhai
   Collaboration: Tongji Architectural Design (Group) Co., Ltd
   Client: Shanghai Xuhui Binjiang Development Investment
   Construction Co.,Ltd.
   Floor Area: 1,100 m²
   Design Period: 2013.04–2013.09
   Completion: 2014.09

36 HUAXIN CONFERENCE HUB
   Location: 142 Tianlin Road, Xuhui District, Shanghai
   Design Team: Chen Yifeng, Liu Yichun, Gao Lin, Wu Zhenghui, Ma Danhong
   Collaboration: Shanghai Architectural Design Research Institute Co., Ltd.
   Client: SVA Real Estate Co.,Ltd.
   Floor Area: 1,000 m²
   Design Period: 2013.07–2015.08
   Completion: 2015.12

Atelier Deshaus   Catalog of Works

37 WEST BUND ART CENTER
   Location: 2555 Longteng Avenue, Xuhui District, Shanghai
   Design Team: Liu Yichun, Chen Yifeng, Wang Longhai,
   Wu Zhenghui, Wang Weishi
   Collaboration: Tongji Architectural Design (Group) Co., Ltd
   Client: Shanghai Xuhui Land Development Co.,Ltd.
   Floor Area: 10,800 m^2
   Design Period: 2014.02–2014.07
   Completion: 2014.09

38 ONE FOUNDATION KINDERGARTEN IN XINCHANG COUNTY
   Location: Xinchang County, Tianquan, Sichuan Province
   Design Team: Chen Yifeng, Liu Yichun, Gao Lin, Gao De
   Collaboration: Beijing Tongcheng Fanhua Construction
   Engineering Consulting Co.,Ltd.
   Client: One Foundation
   Floor Area: 1,500 m^2
   Design Period: 2014.10–2015.04
   Completion: 2017.01

39 ATELIER DESHAUS ON WEST BUND
   Location: 2555–16 Longteng Avenue, Xuhui District, Shanghai
   Design Team: Liu Yichun, Chen Yifeng, Wang Longhai, Wang Weishi
   Collaboration: Tongji Architectural Design (Group) Co., Ltd
   Client: Atelier Deshaus
   Floor Area: 430 m^2
   Design Period: 2014.11–2015.04
   Completion: 2015.11

40 YUNYANG RIVERFRONT VISITOR CENTER
   Location: Binjiang Avenue, Yunyang County, Chongqing
   Design Team: Chen Yifeng, Gao Lin, Song Chongfang, Wang Xuepei
   Collaboration: CMCU Engineering Co., Ltd.
   Client: Immigration Bureau of Yunyang County, Yunyang Urban Development & Investment (Group) Co., Ltd.
   Floor Area: 9,011 m^2
   Design Period: 2015.01–2016.08
   Completion: 2019.10

41 BLOSSOM PAVILION
    Location: 570 West Huaihai Road, Shanghai
    Design Team: Liu Yichun, Wang Longhai, Ding Jieru
    Collaboration: AND Office, Zhan Wang
    Client: Shanghai Urban Sculpture Art Center
    Floor Area: 96 m^2
    Design Period: 2015.04–2015.10
    Completion: 2015.11

42 TAIZHOU CONTEMPORARY ART MUSEUM
    Location: Fengshan Road, Taizhou, Zhejiang Province
    Design Team: Liu Yichun, Chen Yifeng, Shen Wen
    Collaboration: AND Office
    Client: Taizhou Shimao Culture & Innovation Development Co. Ltd.
    Floor Area: 2,454 m^2
    Design Period: 2015.05–2015.09
    Completion: 2019.04

43 MODERN ART MUSEUM AND ITS WALKWAYS
    Location: 4777 Binjiang Avenue, Pudong District, Shanghai
    Design Team: Liu Yichun, Chen Yifeng, Wang Weishi, Shen Wen, Chen Hao, Wang Longhai, Chan Hiongai, Ding Jieru, Zhou Mengdie
    Collaboration: Tongji Architectural Design (Group) Co., Ltd, AND Office
    Client: Shanghai East Bund Investment (Group) Co., Ltd.
    Floor Area: 9,180 m^2
    Design Period: 2015.05–2016.10
    Completion: 2016.12

44 ZHANGJIANG INTERNATIONAL INNOVATION CENTER
    Location: Zhangjiang Hi-tech Park, Pudong District, Shanghai
    Design Team: Chen Yifeng, Gao De, Huang Minkun
    Collaboration: Shanghai Chengkai Construction Design Co.,Ltd.
    Client: Shanghai Yuanfeng Culture Development Co., Ltd.
    Floor Area: 98,980 m^2
    Design Period: 2015.07–2017.08
    Completion: 2017.08

45 THE WATER TANK HOUSE
    Location: Ruijin Road (No. 2), Huangpu District, Shanghaii
    Design Team: Liu Yichun, Liu Kenan, Wang Longhai, Li Ang, Shen Wen, Jiang Yiqing, Zhou Peiyi, Liu Ran, Chang Hongliang, Ke Mingen, Wang Zhili
    Collaboration: Atelier XÜK
    Cllent: Private
    Floor Area: 68 m^2
    Design Period: 2015.07–2015.09

Atelier Deshaus   Catalog of Works

46 HUAZHU HEADQUARTERS
    Location: Plot 0804, Jiangqiao, Jiading District, Shanghai
    Design Team: Liu Yichun, Wang Shuyi, Chen Hao, Shen Wen, Chen Yu,
    Wang Longhai, Wei Wenda, Tang Yun, Wang Jiawen
    Collaboration: East China Architectural Design And Research Institute
    Client: Huazhu Business Management Co.Ltd.
    Floor Area: 84,115 m^2
    Design Period: 2015.8-2019.11
    Completion: 2022 (estimated)

47 TEA HOUSE IN LI GARDEN
    Location: 2555 Longteng Avenue, Xuhui District, Shanghai
    Design Team: Liu Yichun, Shen Wen, Wang Weishi
    Collaboration: AND Office
    Client: Guangdong Fang Suo Culture Investment Development Co.,Ltd.
    Floor Area: 19 m^2
    Design Period: 2015.09-2015.12
    Completion: 2016.06

48 80,000-TON SILOS ART CENTER ON MINSHENG WHARF
    Location: 3 Minsheng Road, Pudong District, Shanghai
    Design Team: Liu Yichun, Chen Yifeng, Chan Hiongai,
    Wang Longhai, Wang Weishi
    Collaboration: Tongji Architectural Design (Group) Co., Ltd, AND Office
    Client: Shanghai East Bund Investment (Group) Co., Ltd.
    Floor Area: 16,322 m^2
    Design Period: 2015.10-2017.10
    Completion: 2017.10

49 FANG SUO BOOK TOWER
    Location: Binjiang Greenland, Pudong District, Shanghai
    Design Team: Liu Yichun, Zhou Mengdie, Wang Longhai, Chan Hiongai
    Collaboration: AND Office, Shanghai Municipal Engineering
    Design Institute Co., Ltd.
    Client: Shanghai Fang Suo Culture Investment Development Co.,Ltd.
    Floor Area: 8,000 m^2
    Design Period: 2015.10-2018.12
    Completion: 2019.12

50 PUDONG ART MUSEUM
    Location: Lujiazui, Pudong District, Shanghai
    Design Team: Liu Yichun, Chen Yifeng, Wang Longhai, Nan Xu, Shen
    Wen, Wang Weishi, Zhou Mengdie, Ding Jieru, Chen Hao
    Client: Shanghai Lujiazu (Group) Co., Ltd.
    Floor Area: 28,500 m^2
    Design Period: 2015.11-2016.02

51 QINTAI ART MUSEUM
   Location: Zhiyin Avenue, Hanyang District, Wuhan, Hubei Province
   Design Team: Liu Yichun, Chen Yu, Wang Longhai, Hu Chenchen, Chen Hao, Shen Wen, Chen Chihhan, Tang Yun, Zhang Xiaoqi, Wu Wenchao, Deng Rui, Liu Xin, Pang Zirui, Wang Jiawen, Cao Ye
   Collaboration: Wuhan Architectural Design Institute
   Client: Wuhan City Construction Group Co., Ltd.
   Floor Area: 43,000 m^2
   Design Period: 2016.05–2018.09
   Completion: 2021.12

52 UPPER CLOISTER ON JINSHAN (GOLDEN) MOUNTAIN
   Location: Jinshan Mountain, Beijing
   Design Team: Liu Yichun, Shen Wen, Chan Hiongai, Wang Longhai, Gong Yu, Zhang Xiaoqi, Wang Yi, Sun Huizhong
   Collaboration: Beijing Yanhuang United Construction Design Co.,Ltd.
   Client: Chengde Aranya Real Estate Development Co., Ltd.
   Floor Area: 615 m^2
   Design Period: 2016.11–2018.03
   Completion: 2022 (estimated)

53 NOVARTIS CAMPUS PHASE II (NOMINATED)
   Location: 4218 Jinke Road, Pudong District, Shanghai
   Design Team: Liu Yichun, Chen Hao, Hu Chenchen, Chan Hiongai
   Client: Novartis International AG
   Floor Area: 15,749 m^2
   Design Period: 2017.01- 2018.03

54 HOUSE ATO
   Location: South Piazza of the National Stadium
   Design Team: Liu Yichun, Shen Wen, Deng Rui, Gong Yu
   Collaboration: AND Office
   Client: China House Vision Curation Committee
   Floor Area: 160 m^2
   Design Period: 2017.01–2018.04
   Completion: 2018.09

55 WEST BUND LIBRARY
   Location: 1 West Longhua Road, Xuhui District, Shanghai
   Design Team: Liu Yichun, Chan Hiongai, Xu Haotian, Deng Rui, Wang Jiawen
   Collaboration: Atelier Z+
   Historic Preservation Consultant: East China Architectural Design & Research Institute Co., Ltd.
   Client: Shanghai West Bund Development (Group) Co., Ltd.
   Floor Area: 8,667 m^2
   Design Period: 2017.08-

56 JINXI HIGH SCHOOL IN KUNSHAN
   Location: Jinfu Road, Kunshan, Jiangsu Province
   Design Team: Chen Yifeng, Gao Lin, Ma Danhong, Tang Dazhou,
   Song Chongfang, Wang Yiling, Xie Jingyi, Du Shangfang, Gao De,
   Cai Mian, Huang Minkun
   Collaboration: Tongji Architectural Design (Group) Co., Ltd.
   Client: Kunshan Education Bureau
   Floor Area: 72,000 m^2
   Design Period: 2017.09–2022.02

57 BRIDGE IN JINSHAN MOUNTAIN
   Location: Jinshan Mountain, Beijing
   Design Team: Liu Yichun, Chan Hiongai
   Collaboration: AND Office
   Client: Chengde Aranya Real Estate Development Co., Ltd.
   Span: 33 m
   Design Period: 2017.10–2018.05
   Completion: 2021.08

58 RIVERSIDE PASSAGE
   Location: 2524 Yangshupu Rd,
   Yangshupu Gas Factory Wharf, Yangpu, Shanghai
   Planning: Atelier Z+, Atelier Liu Yuyang Architects, Atelier Deshaus
   Structural Design: AND Office
   Design Team: Liu Yichun, Shen Wen, Chan Hiongai
   Coordination: Zhang Bin, Wang Weijie, Wang Jiaqi, Guo Yifeng
   Landscape Consultant: YIYU Design, Laurent Landscape&Architects Firm
   Floor Area: 268 m^2
   Design Period: 2018.03–2018.11
   Completion: 2019.10

59 SCIENCE PAVILION OF GEOLOGY IN JIANGSU HORTI PARK
   Location: Science Pavilion of Geology in Jiangsu Horti Park
   Design Team: Liu Yichun, Shen Wen, Chen Yu, Chan Hiongai,
   Zhang Xiaoqi, Wang Yi, Chen Yuwei, Chen Chihhan
   Collaboration: Nanjing Yangtze River Urban Architectural Design Co., Ltd.
   Client: Jiangsu Yuanboyuan Construction & Development Co., Ltd.
   Floor Area: 1,500 m^2
   Design Period: 2018.10–2019.10
   Completion: 2021.05

60 BAICHA TOWN HALL
   Location: Xilong County, Anji, Zhejiang Province
   Design Team: Liu Yichun, Xu Haotian, Wang Shuyi, Chan Hiongai, Chen Xu
   Collaboration: East China Architectural Design And Research Institute
   Client: Anji Xushan Culture Co., Ltd.
   Floor Area: 1,942 m²
   Design Period: 2019.05–2020.02
   Completion: 2022 (estimated)

61 SHANGMAKAN MUSEUM AND BAICHA MUSEUM IN ANJI
   Location: Xilong County, Anji, Zhejiang Province
   Design Team: Liu Yichun, Wang Zhuohao, Wang Shuyi, Shen Wen, Chan Hiongai, Chen Yuwei, Chen Xu, Chen Chihhan, Tang Yun, Cao Ye
   Collaboration: East China Architectural Design And Research Institute
   Client: Anji Xushan Culture Co., Ltd.
   Floor Area: 7,000 m²
   Design Period: 2019.05–2020.06
   Completion: 2022 (estimated)

62 RENOVATION OF 190 WUYI ROAD
   Location: Plot D2-8 22/1 Huayang Road, Changning District, Shanghai
   Design Team: Liu Yichun, Chen Yu, Wang Shuyi, Wang Yi, Wei Wenda
   Collaboration: Shanghai Construction & Design Research Institute Co., Ltd.
   Client: Shanghai Jiaxi Real Estate Development Co., Ltd.
   Floor Area: 19,295 m²
   Design Period: 2019.08
   Completion: 2023 (estimated)

63 LUJIA NO.2 MIDDLE SCHOOL IN KUNSHAN
   Location: Lujia Town, Kunshan, Jiangsu Province
   Design Team: Chen Yifeng, Ma Danhong, Gao De, Xie Jingyi, Liang Jun, Du Shangfang, Jin Yilei
   Collaboration: Tongji Architectural Design (Group) Co., Ltd.
   Client: the People's Government of Lujia, Kunshan
   Floor Area: 35,000 m²
   Design Period: 2019.11

64 ARANYA INNOVATION AND ART CENTER
   Location: Beidaihe New District, Qinhuangdao, Hebei Province
   Design Team: Liu Yichun, Shen Wen, Wang Shuyi, Zhang Xiaoqi, Chen Xu, Wang Zhuohao, Zhang Yichen | Collaboration: AND Office, Qsinghua Architectural Design Research Co., Ltd., Atelier and I
   Floor Area: 11,000 m²
   Design Period: 2019.11–2021.02
   Completion: 2022 (estimated)

65 YANGLIUQING GRAND CANAL NATIONAL CULTURE PARK
(FIRST PLACE OF THE COMPETITION)
Location: Yuanbaodao, Xiqing District, Tianjin
Design Team: Liu Yichun, Chen Hao, Hu Chenchen, Xu Haotian, Chen Xu,
Chen Yuwei, Wang Zhuohao, Wang Jiawen
Collaboration: Nippon Design Center, Inc., Li Ronghui
Client: the People's Government of Xiqing District, Tianjin
Floor Area: 76,000 m^2
Design Period: 2020.05

66 VISITOR CENTER OF WULINMEN PORT
(FIRST PLACE OF THE COMPETITION)
Location: Huanchengbei Road, Xiacheng District, Hangzhou, Zhejiang Province
Design Team: Chen Yifeng, Gao Lin, Song Chongfang, Wang Yiling,
Xie Jingyi, Du Shangfang
Collaboration: Zhejiang University Architectural Design Research Co., Ltd.
Client: Hangzhou Canal Comprehensive Protection And Development
Construction Group Co., Ltd.
Floor Area: 20,252 m^2 (park), 851 m^2 (building)
Design Period: 2020.09–2021.09

67 HAINAN ART MUSEUM (FIRST PLACE OF THE COMPETITION)
Location: South to the Wenmingdong Tunnel, Haikou, Hainan Province
Design Team: Liu Yichun, Chan Hiongai, Wang Zhuohao, Chen Xu, Chen
Yuwei, Zhang Jianing, Wang Shuyi, Zhang Xiaoqi, Ji Hongliang, Li Jie,
Liu Xin, Wang Longhai
Collaboration: Tongji Architectural Design (Group) Co., Ltd.
Client: Haikou Tourism & Culture Investment Group Co., Ltd.
Floor Area: 35,364 m^2
Design Period: 2020.10–

68 ZHANGJIAGANG ART MUSEUM
Location: East to Yiganhe Road, Zhangjianggang, Jiangsu Province
Design Team: Liu Yichun, Shen Wen, Zhang Xiaoqi, Chen Xu, Shi Yujie,
Sun Huizhong
Collaboration: AND Office, Arts Group Co., Ltd.
Client: Zhangjiagang Municipal Bureau of Style, Radio,
Television and Tourism
Floor Area: 18,000 m^2
Design Period: 2020.11–

ATELIER DESHAUS

Founded in 2001, Atelier Deshaus was one of the first independent architectural studios in China. Principal architects Liu Yichun and Chen Yifeng were born in 1969 and 1972. They both graduated from Tongji University with a master's degree in architecture.

EXHIBITIONS

Atelier Deshaus has been invited to participate in many international architecture and art exhibitions in more than fifteen countries and regions. These include *Alors, La Chine?* at Center Pompidou in 2003, *E-W/N-S* at Arc en Reve Center d'Architecture in Bordeaux in 2004, *China Contemporary* at Netherlands Architecture Institute in Rotterdam in 2006, *China Design Now* at the V&A Museum in London in 2008, *ARCHITopia* at CIVA in Brussels in 2008, *Positions* Portrait of a New Generation of Chinese Architects at La Cite de l'architecture et du patrimoine in Paris in 2008, *New Chinese Architecture* at CA'ASI Art Gallery for the Biennale Architettura 2010, *From Research to Design* at Triennale di Milano in 2012, *Eastern Promises* at the MAK Austrian Museum of Applied Arts in 2013, the London Design Museum in 2015, *ZAI XING TU MU: Sixteen Chinese Galleries and Fifteen Chinese Architects* at the 2016 Aedas Architecture Forum in Berlin, and *Reuse, Renew, Recycle: Recent Architecture from China* at MoMA in New York in 2021.

AWARDS

Atelier Deshaus was regarded as the "2011 Design Vanguard" by *Architectural Record*, and was awarded second prize in the 2010 New Chinese Architecture competition by AS Architecture Studio. The Long Museum West Bund, directed by Liu, won the *Architectural Review* Award for Emerging Architecture in 2014. It was also nominated for Designs of the Year 2015 by London Design Museum and was named Best of Best in the Iconic Awards 2015 by German Design Council that same year. It was awarded the Gold Prize of the ASC Architecture Creation Awards for Public Architecture in 2016, the Honor Award Best in Show for Architecture 2019 by AIA's China Chapter and won Gold Prize at the 2020 ARCASIA Awards for Architecture in the "Public Amenity: Social and Cultural Buildings" category. Liu Yichun was regarded as the most influential designer of the year in 2015 by Forbes and architect of the year in 2019 by UED.

YUNG HO CHANG
Yung Ho Chang, FAIA, is principal architect of Atelier FCJZ and Professor of Practice at MIT Architecture.

LI XIANGNING
Dr. Li Xiangning is dean and full professor in history, theory and criticism at Tongji University College of Architecture and Urban Planning. He is a member of CICA (Comité International des Critiques d'Architecture), and secretary general of the China Architectural Society Architectural Criticism Committee. He is editor-in-chief of the international magazine *Architecture China*.

LI SHIQIAO
Li Shiqiao is Weedon Professor in Asian Architecture at the University of Virginia. He is an internationally recognized scholar whose research is focused on understanding emergent conditions in Chinese cities by contextualizing them in traditional intellectual discourses, and in conceptions of modernity in architecture in their Western and Asian manifestations.

CO-FOUNDERS & PRINCIPAL ARCHITECTS:
Liu Yichun, Chen Yifeng
Zhuang Shen (2001–2009)

TEAM MEMBERS (LISTED IN ORDER OF JOINING THE COMPANY)
Gao Lin, Wang Longhai, Wang Shuyi, Li Jun, Song Chongfang, Gao De, Shen Wen, Zheng Yi, Chan Hiongai, Ma Danhong, Zhang Xiaoqi, Wang Yiling, Wang Yi, Wei Wenda, Chen Yu, Chen Yuwei, Song Yangliu, Chen Xu, Xie Jingyi, Tang Yun, Dong Sichao, Zhang Wenyi, Liu Xin, Wang Zhuohao, Zhang Jianing, Li Jie, Ji Hongliang, Shi Yujie, Du Shangfang, Sun Huizhong, Gong Yu, Liang Jun, Zhou Chuxi, Cao Ye

FORMER TEAM MEMBERS
Tang Yu, He Yangsong, He Wangpan, Qian Lin, Fan Minji, Chen Jiang, Ye Ying, Wu Di, Ye Ang, Zhang Yi, Qiao Yuting, Peng Xu, Song Yuhui, Yang Shuting, Chen Juan, Peng Xiangge, Li Jun, He Yong, Zhou Jing, Yang Baoxin, Zhang Xu, Zhu Feng, Dou Yinian, Huang Dong, Wang Yue, Liu Qian, Zhang Jieliang, Fan Beilei, Ren Hao, Qiu Mei, Xing Jiabei, Wu Zhenghui, Sun Yuanting, Zuo Long, Wang Xuepei, Wang Zimu, Wu Wenchao, Yan Xiaohuan, Huang Minkun, Ding Jieru, Huang Ying, Xue Shu, Chen Hao, Hu Chenchen, Nan Xu, Deng Rui, Tang Dazhou, Zhou Mengdie, Wang Weishi, Cai Mian, Lv Shiyang, Feng Zhentao, Pan Ling, Xu Haotian, Jin Yilei, Chen Chihhan, Wang Jiawen, Pang Zirui, Tong Zekun, Zhang Yicheng

Unless otherwise noted, all images are courtesy and copyright © Atelier Deshaus

Chen Hao: 9(t), 109, 115, 116(t,b), 117(t), 120, 121, 137, 138-139, 159(t), 239, 240, 245, 247, 249, 250-251; Liu Yichun: 9(b), 25, 26, 27(t), 79(t), 99, 198(t), 200, 239; Jin Sisi: 14; Su Shengliang: 25(b), 29(b), 81, 82-83, 84, 85, 86, 87, 88, 89, 91, 92, 93, 94, 95, 96-97, 101, 106(b), 107, 122-123, 124, 126, 128-129, 132, 133, 143, 144, 145, 146-147, 149, 152-153, 205, 206(t), 209(t), 210-211, 214, 215(b), 228, 229; Tian Fangfang: 27(b), 100, 135(br), 156, 157, 163, 164-165, 166, 167, 168, 169, 172, 173, 174-175, 177, 178, 179, 180-181, 183, 184, 185, 188-189, 191, 192, 193, 195, 196-197, 198(b), 199, 201, 202, 203, 206(b), 208, 209(b), 215(t), 216, 217, 218, 219, 220-221, 222, 224, 225, 226, 227, 228, 229, 231, 235, 242-243, 244, 246, 248; Zhan Wang (artist): 27(t), 155; Zhang Siye: 37, 39, 41, 42, 43; Shu He: 45, 48-49, 50, 51, 53, 54, 58, 59, 60-61, 73, 75(t), 76-77; Yao Li: 63, 64-65, 66, 67, 68, 70, 71, 74, 75(b), 79(b); Walter Mair (CH): 102-103, 104, 108, 112-113, 209(t), 210-211, 214, 215(b); Xia Zhi: 106(t); Eiichi Kano:116(m), 117(b), 118-119; Zhou Dingqi: 159(b), 160-161; Wu Qingshan: 232-233, 234, 236

Every reasonable effort has been made to acknowledge the ownership of copyright for photographs included in this volume. Any errors that may have occurred are inadvertent, and will be corrected in subsequent editions provided that notification is sent in writing to the publisher.

ATELIER DESHAUS
2001–2020

FOREWORD by Yung Ho Chang
ESSAYS by Li Xiangning, Li Shiqiao

EDITOR
Li Xiangning

PROJECT SUPPORT
Hubertus Adam

TRANSLATIONS
Zhou Ying (essay by Li Xiangning)
Zhou Ying, Jiang Jiawei
(project descriptions)

PLAN EDITING
Zhang Wenyi, Tong Zekun

GRAPHIC CONCEPT / DESIGN
Klaus Stille Studio, Zheng Yi

PRINTING
Artron Art (Group) Co., Ltd.

PAPER
120gsm Munken Lynx ID
115gsm Arctic Volume White

PUBLISHER
Park Books
Niederdorfstrasse 54
8001 Zurich
Switzerland
www.park-books.com

© 2022 Atelier Deshaus and Park Books AG, Zurich

Park Books is being supported by the Federal Office of Culture with a general subsidy for the years 2021–2024.

All rights reserved; no part of this publication may be reproduced, stored in a retrieval system or transmitted in any form or by any means, electronic, mechanical, photocopying, recording, or otherwise, without the prior written consent of the publisher.

ISBN 978-3-03860-223-1